On The Fast Track

Also by Kimberly Quinn Smith, MA—*Striving for the Purple Heart-mothers in the universal pursuit of honor*

On The Fast Track

◆

Teens Getting Too Much Too Soon In These Rapidly Changing And Uncertain Times, And What Parents Can Do To Stay Connected

By Kimberly Quinn Smith, MA

Illustrated by Ryan, Caitlin, Aidan, Shannon, and Delaney Smith
Cover Design by Caitlin Kennedy Smith

iUniverse, Inc.
New York Lincoln Shanghai

On The Fast Track
Teens Getting Too Much Too Soon In These Rapidly Changing And Uncertain Times, And What Parents Can Do To Stay Connected

iUniverse books may be ordered through booksellers or by contacting:

iUniverse
2021 Pine Lake Road, Suite 100
Lincoln, NE 68512
www.iuniverse.com
1-800-Authors (1-800-288-4677)

ISBN-13: 978-0-595-36561-6 (pbk)
ISBN-13: 978-0-595-80992-9 (ebk)
ISBN-10: 0-595-36561-2 (pbk)
ISBN-10: 0-595-80992-8 (ebk)

Printed in the United States of America

This book is dedicated to Casey,
my beach buddy and fellow sunrise appreciater,
and to all of the Casey's the world over…

Contents

Part IV   *Teens Slipping Through The Cracks*

-the connection to disconnection

Part V   *Parents and the Road Less Traveled*

Part VI   *On Staying Connected Through These Challenging Years...*

Acknowledgements

I would first like to thank my husband Tom and my five children for being so supportive of this project. Their constant inquiries as far as my progress were heart warming and inspired me to move forward at times when things seemed overwhelming. Even in the midst of baseball season, I was able to return to the moment with my writing and experience the true joy that it provides. I would like to thank the computer geniuses who made this book a reality. I am grateful for the combined efforts of Roberta Cota, Jonathan Griffin, Roger Torres, and Sue Kelly-Harkey. I am grateful to Rolf Anderson for designing and creating my web-site. His natural talent and creative energy made it possible to accurately express our flavor as a family, my interests as an author and parenting skills educator, as well as describing the content of my books. Thank you also to the Hazen's Notch Foundation for providing seemingly endless miles of heavenly cross-country skiing trails. My brief escapes into the blissful solitude of the woods allowed my creative energy to flow and ideas to emerge. For this I am deeply grateful. I would also like to express appreciation to the young adults and professionals whom I interviewed. I enjoyed each and every one of their life stories and learned from their professional expertise. I am grateful for the efforts and artwork of my illustrators Ryan, Caitlin, Aidan, Shannon, and Delaney Smith. I would also like to thank my sister, an author and journalist, for her continued efforts to support this project while under the pressure to complete her own, as well as for her enthusiasm and optimism. I was able to benefit not only from her encouragement, but from her extensive knowledge of the writing/publishing world. I would also like to thank my dear friend of twenty years, Dr. David Landers, for his knowledge, support, and assistance with the *Boys to Men* Chapter. To Casey, wherever you are, thank you for being the voice for young males everywhere who have gone unheard, unnoticed, and who are unable to express their thoughts, fears, and anxieties about approaching manhood during these confusing and uncertain times. It is my hope that your courage will reach the many young males out there who yearn to be able to do the same. Thank you.

Foreword

It is amazing how things can be meant to be, when something happens, or lands in your lap that kind of pulls everything together. As I write this foreword, I am only a few pages short of finishing up this book. In fact, I didn't even intend to write a foreword until I met my new friend Casey this morning. I had strolled out of our annually rented condo on a beach in Maryland to watch the sunrise. It was barely 5:00 am as I sat there in my jammies wiggling my bare feet in the sand. I looked over to my right and noticed a teenager staring off across the ocean. He was all by himself. I looked to my left and saw that there were only a few scattered sunrise appreciaters in that direction as well. The beach was basically wide open, serene and peaceful. Before I knew it, my new soon-to-be beach buddy had parked himself next to me. His name was Casey and he had just graduated from high school. He told me that he had come here with his friends for *Senior Week*, and that he had wanted for all of them to watch the sunrise with him but they were all still sleeping. My gang was still fast asleep in the condo also so Casey and I watched the sunrise together.

It didn't take me long to figure out that my eighteen-year-old friend was more self-aware than most middle-aged adults, a real *old soul* as they say. To begin with, Casey appreciated a sunrise. This alone was very telling of his personality, especially as he was a teenager. He started off telling me about how what he liked most about life were the simple things, and that he felt that we, as Americans, have gotten greedy, always wanting more. He said that in a way, he had wished that he had been a teenager in the 50's or 60's when things seemed "less complicated." He talked about 911 and how scared he was sitting in his classroom as a high school freshman when he had first found out. He remembered not understanding what it meant for America and the future. Casey told me that it is difficult to look forward to the future because there is so much uncertainty in the world and that no one really knows what is going to happen.

As the sky showed its first glimmer of pink on the horizon, he talked about how scary it was to just graduate from high school as his whole routine up until now has been waking up in the morning and going to school. This routine that he had been doing for the last twelve years plus kindergarten had now come to an end and he said to me, "It's like, now what?" When I asked him what some of the other kids in his graduating class were doing, he had a lot to say. He told me that some were going to college, and that twelve kids (all males) had enlisted in the military, four in the marines and the rest in the army. He told me that the reason they had enlisted was because "they take care of you. They give you food, and housing, and money for college. It's not a bad deal really, except the part where you may have to risk your life." Then Casey said, "I would sign up in a minute if I felt that our country was threatened or in immediate danger, like it was in World War I and II with the hit on Pearl Harbor and all that. This right here, sitting on the beach is worth fighting for. I think that very few kids my age think about our ancestors and what they did to secure this freedom, the fighting and the courage that it took for us to be able to sit on the beach like this and watch the sunrise. They take this all for granted, but I don't. I am grateful for the freedom to watch the sunrise. There is no where else I would want to live. I think this is the best country in the world. I just don't think that very many kids think about these things, but I do. I am proud to be an American and I would fight for my country in a second. It just bothers me that kids are over in the Middle East fighting over oil. It's all about money. To risk your life for money and oil, that's different, that's crazy."

While on the topic of money, Casey then went on to talk about his grandparents and how he loved to sit and "listen for hours" about stories from "the day." They talked about the prices of bread and milk and the goings on in the 50's. Then he said, "kids don't appreciate grandparents enough either. I could sit and listen to their stories all day. They know so much and they have so many interesting stories to tell." He talked about how he felt that the focus on money has gotten "way out of hand. There are kids out there driving around in fifty thousand dollar cars while there are kids in other countries like Africa walking around in rags and without shoes. Not only that but there is so much disease. They don't get how rich we are over here. It just seems like we have all gotten out of touch and greedy."

Casey told me that he likes the simple things in life, but that he is well aware that the world does revolve around money to some degree and that he has some anxiety about going out into the world. He informed me that he had already enrolled in a tech school for the coming fall semester to learn to be an auto mechanic as he has always enjoyed working with his hands and he knows that he "will always have a job." Casey also explained to me that he had struggled through high school as he "had ADD and it was a challenge to be somewhere and to be expected to do things when there was only one method of learning." He said, "I'm bright. It's just that I learn in a different way than other kids. That's all, and because they only teach the mainstream way it was hard for me. I barely made it through." He told me that his memory of high school could be summed up in one word, "worksheets." My beach buddy then explained to me that, "It would make more sense to teach a class called Real Life 101, where kids are taught how to handle things and how to survive out here in the world. We get out of high school and have no idea what to do about anything. We don't know about taxes or any of that real life stuff."

The part where my chance meeting with Casey being meant to be became even more overtly obvious was when he began talking about what it meant to him to be male in today's world and the pressure he feels to be successful. The information he was freely giving me up until this point had already captured my attention, but I became even more focused when he began to talk about gender related issues as the only chapter I have left to finish is *Boys to Men-what it means to be male in today's world and how they get there.* I put this chapter off as I was overwhelmed with what young men are dealing with today, as well as the fact that I have never been male myself and therefore did not even have a personal reference point with which to begin.

The sun, at this point, had risen and resembled a hot pink super-ball. We sat there, mutually in awe of its beauty. I then asked Casey what he thought it meant to be a man, meaning a *healthy* man. He told me that what he wanted most of all was to be a good father and a good husband. He said that, "I feel a little weird thinking about this stuff, especially since I'm only eighteen and I'm here on Senior Week, but I do. It is sort of always in the back of my mind. Of course, there is the pressure to get a good job and make enough money to have kids. But mainly I think that being a good father has do with being there for your kids. That's the main thing. You have to be there for your kids. I want to play sports with them and read them bedtime stories. I didn't have a dad there to take me fishing or to tell me things about growing up from being a boy to becoming a man. I didn't have anyone there to talk about how to treat a girlfriend. I know that I am only eighteen, but it has affected me in my relationships with girls. I feel like I mess up a lot because I don't know what to do. Fathers are supposed to walk you through, and tell you how to treat a woman right and to show you how to be a man. Without a father around, how are you supposed to know what to do or what it means to be a man...I am going to make sure that this doesn't happen to my kids. I'm going to be there for them so they don't have to feel this way, so scared and so unsure about what's next and what to do." As he said this, I glanced over at my fellow sunrise appreciater and noticed a tear streaming down his left cheek.

Introduction

O.K., so now what? It seems that I have a little more time on my hands. I tell my kids to go take a shower and they do. I don't have to wash anybody's hair or be a bathroom lifeguard, sitting on the edge of the toilet ready to prevent a possible concussion or drowning. My kids are all self-sufficient. Nobody wears diapers and they still want to go on family vacations and hold my hand in public. Life is good.

Welcome to *Stage Two*, the in be "tween" stage, where no formula, diapers or purred carrots exist. In fact, I wish that I could freeze-frame this stage and stay right here forever. There are no desires to go to dances, no one is old enough to drive or to know anyone who can drive, the hostile hormones have not quite kicked in yet (though they are on simmer ready to emerge in the not too distant future), and I can still rule with an eyebrow. Not only that, but my children are still willing to give me hugs and let me kiss them goodnight. I am thinking that this is a good place to be. I like this stage. If only it would last forever.

Then as if leaving the warmth and comfort of the womb, our little darlings leave elementary school and enter a new dimension…middle school. As parents, it is as if we are driving along on a sunny day enjoying the ride, the music, the scenery. If the kids act up in the back seat, we can threaten to pull the car over and it still works. They panic at the wrath in our voice and fear that we may continue to drive past McDonald's if they do not follow orders. The kids quiet down and we continue to enjoy our quality family time together. We jump back into the conversation we are having with our partner. Life is good. All of the sudden, the sky grows dark and the wind picks up. The conversation comes to a halt as we need our immediate attention to be on the road in front of us. A deer jumps out in front of us. We serve to miss it and lose control of the wheel. The combination of the dirt road and the rain has caused us to hydroplane. The kids sense that we are losing control and begin to act out in the back seat. We turn the wheel into the curve and the car begins to straighten itself out. We slow down and take a deep breath. Our heart is pumping fast and furiously. The road is getting windier and bumpier. Maybe we should go back the way we came. We look in the rear-view mirror and see that the wind has brought a tree down across the road behind us. It's getting darker. No matter what, we cannot let on that we are nervous as it will only cause the kids to become anxious. They need to know that we've got it all under control. We may need to fake it. I think we can pull it off.

As difficult as it may be for us as parents to navigate through the dark and bumpy middle school years, it is infinitely more challenging and often painful, for our tweens and teens to muddle their way through these confusing, tumultuous years. They can taste autonomy just around the corner but it is un-pioneered territory, and as excited as they may *appear* to be about growing up, they are also terrified at the same time. Just as with anything else, fear stems from the unknown. It is this duality of having one hand striving to be independent and the other one reaching for a teddy bear to sleep with at night that causes such turbulence within the tween.

With every day that goes by, their friends become more important to them and begin to influence the decisions they make from what to wear to how to blow smoke rings. Our children are scared and so are we as everything we have ever taught them is put to a test. They have entered the fog of pre-adolescence and they are feeling their way through it with their eyes opened wide and their hands out in front of them, in order to figure out who they are and what their place in this world is. They are beginning to have their very first thoughts and feelings in regards to their sexuality, not only as far as how to interact on a new level with the opposite (or the same) gender, but they are also simply trying to figure out how to *be* male or female. These feelings may become more complicated if the child finds himself or herself being attracted to or having dreams about the same gender. They may question whether they can or should keep it a secret for fear of how the family and peers will react.

Both boys and girls become conscious of their physiques, not only in regards to weight, but muscle size and tone as well. In fact, male eating disorders are now on the rise as boys become equally obsessed with impressing their peers. These tweens become ultra-observant of their surroundings and the people in their lives. As quickly as they change a t-shirt, they are trying on new personas to see which one fits best and feels the most comfortable. Their fragile self-esteem very vulnerably picks up the most subtle of cues as we mirror how they perceive themselves by how we respond to their thoughts, feelings, and behavior on a daily basis. Inside they are very confused and unsure about what is next and they are desperately searching for solid ground. This of course explains why suicide is so common amongst teens. Of course, genetics and socioeconomic situations also play a role, but there is a significant amount of undisputed evidence that suggests that these children are at high risk for depression and suicide due to the extreme emotional turbulence, confusion, and insecurity that they are feeling. It is also possible for us to forget on occasion, especially if they are towering over us, that they *are* children, and very much so.

Our middleschoolers are slowly trying to wiggle out of and shed their elementary skin as it no longer fits, although their new skin does not exactly fit either, at least not as comfortably as their old skin did. It feels different and they are trying to get used to it. They notice that the other kids wearing this skin seem to like certain music and like specific brands of clothes and sneakers. It didn't seem to matter much before. They talk older, too. They'll definitely have to make sure that the door is shut when they go home and play with their Barbies or Match Box cars after school. These tweens become aware of their own family's socioeconomic situation and begin to compare themselves to other kids as far as what they have, where they live, and what their parents do. Independent thinking is probably the biggest challenge for the tween as fitting in with the group is the most important thing in his or her world right now.

Then all of the sudden it happens, we leave the *Tween Stage* and the demons of full-blown adolescence take over. Now we really begin to feel the heat. The pressure is on. Every parenting skill we have developed and used successfully, for the most part, is about to be put to the test. We have to somehow try to figure out the delicate balance between letting go and tightening the reins when they need us to. Our fear begins to escalate as we think about all of the external variables out in that big world, mainly smoking, drinking, drugs, and unprotected sex. Then there is the driving issue. Inexperienced children with overwhelming feelings of invincibility, a yearning to bust free from parental control and impress friends, are enough to scare anyone. Add alcohol to the mix and we may consider tying them all up in the basement until they are ready to go to college.

For the rest of the journey it will feel as if we have a blind fold on and one hand tied behind our back. We will experience an invasion of the body snatchers with our own eyes and within the comfort of our own homes. It is almost as if from out of no where we hear a voice coming from a loud speaker. It says, "Make sure your seat belt is securely fastened, that your shoulder harness is pulled down tightly, and that your feet are flat against the floor." We look around to see the faces of the other parents, how they are handling their fears and anxieties about the ride they are about to go on. Some have a bit of a tight look. Some are looking straight ahead afraid to move or acknowledge what is in their peripheral vision, and one is as white as a sheet, pasty, and trembling. They wish they could get off the ride and sneak out the exit without being noticed but it is too late. The shoulder harnesses just made that loud locking sound and we feel a slight bit of movement from underneath. The voice comes back on the speaker and says, "This ride involves two corkscrews and three drops over 300 feet. At times your sense of gravity and vertigo may be completely thrown off. There will also be times when you are completely upside down and riding at speeds which may exceed 83 miles per hour. Brace yourselves for the most exciting and terrifying ride we have to offer as you enter *the hormone zone*." We look around and notice that a lot of the parents on the ride have closed their eyes, some are looking straight ahead, and the one who had that white and pasty look has already thrown up.

PART I
The Middle School Years

1

Educational Changes and How They Affect the Tween

It is certainly a change for our kids when they leave the nurturing, very sheltered environment of elementary school to enter the *tween/teen world* of middle school. They are leaving the building and playground that they have grown to know and become comfortable with, and for many kids this change has landed them on the opposite side of town. Kids who live in some of the most rural parts of the country may even find themselves being bussed long distances to larger regional middle schools and being mixed with other kids from all of the other small towns within the designated mileage radius. For some this means leaving fourth grade to enter a school which includes grades five through eight, and for some it means leaving sixth grade to enter a junior high school which is sometimes merged with grades nine through twelve. Either way, these kids went from being the "top dogs" in their school to being on the low end of the teen food chain, and in most cases is quite a huge adjustment. They are also making the transition from a contained classroom where they had the same teacher every day, to a *team* or *cluster* where they change classrooms and have an individual schedule they need to follow. This transition is not a gradual one. Last they knew they were having a class Valentine's Day Party where parents made homemade cookies and they exchanged Barbie and Harry Potter Valentine's. Now they are being shown puberty videos and wondering if anyone is going to ask them to the dance on Friday night.

Michele A. Hernandez writes in *The Middle School Years* that, "the hardest adjustment for young children is the transition from having the same teacher all day (as most do in elementary school) to having a different teacher for every subject (the norm in middle school). More than any other factor, this dramatic procedural change marks the transition from the comforting environment of elementary school to the often 'sink-or-swim' environment of middle school." Hernandez continues to explain that "children love predictability and regularity," and that "for years they have been accustomed to having the same person to teach them each day." These children have gotten used to this one teacher's way of doing things. When they step off the bus each day, they see his or her familiar face, and they know what to expect. They know the routine. Then, Ruiz says, "Suddenly, at the onset of sixth grade, students may find themselves in a different location, while at the same time their routine is completely disrupted. Not only do they have a different teacher for every subject, they also have to move physically from classroom to classroom-the teachers do not come to them. Add to that the confusion of five different ways of assigning homework in the best cases; that is, assuming each of the teachers is consistent in using the same technique every day." She asks, "Is it any wonder, then, that many children who were doing fine in elementary school find themselves lost and confused when they get to middle school?"

As far as academic problems go, she states that roughly 80% of the parents she surveyed said that, "their children's most serious problem was a total lack of organizational skills: how to organize a locker, a backpack, a notebook, or a schedule." Of course, at the middle school level more opportunities begin to present themselves as far as sports, clubs, and various other extra-curricular activities. Just to complicate things a little more, developmentally, these kids are just barely beginning to acquire a concept of time, and are now receiving strong messages from every direction that they need to learn to manage it well if they are going to succeed. Many times, these messages are in the form of consequences, and are often negative. These kids have gone from having a page of homework per night in most cases, to the significantly increased academic workload of middle school or junior high. When homework is not completed there is usually a consequence, whether it means staying after school or attending restricted study hall. Some school athletic programs have rules about grade point averages, and students who are unable to maintain the minimum G.P.A. are not allowed to participate on a sports team. Some students are prevented from going on field trips or attending dances if their work is not turned in. This can be an enormous amount of pressure for a student leaving their elementary comfort zone where there were far fewer expectations and they didn't have to be "so grown up."

Hernandez states that the more time she spends in schools, that "the more clear it is that a student who learns to be a master of his own schedule is much more likely to succeed than an equally bright student who is organizationally impaired." She goes on to say that, "when your children make the transition from fifth to sixth grade (or from sixth to seventh grade), it is perfectly okay as parents to help them organize themselves and teach them the necessary skills." Hernandez talks about the importance of a "homework notebook" and she recommends that parents "organize the notebook *with* him (not *for* him) so that you can train him well and leave him with a lifetime of good study skills and habits." She continues to explain that, "once you have taken the time to set up this notebook with your child, the important part of the routine is to check it every day for the first week of school to make sure that your child is in fact writing down every assignment. As far as getting around the age-old "but Mom, I don't have any homework" fabrication, Hernandez suggests that parents "have their child write in 'No homework' rather than just leaving the space blank. That way you can at least check with a particular teacher if you see a pattern of not writing down homework." Hernandez sums up with, "although setting up a homework notebook seems simple," that she can "almost guarantee that children who get into the habit of keeping close track of all assignments early on will be much more successful students than those who rely on memory or on asking other students in class."

According to Krish and Hannigan, authors of *Those Middle School years: Motivation and achievement begin at home,* "Experts agree that parental involvement at home is consistently associated with higher student motivation and achievement. Armed with a little knowledge of what to look for and how to proceed, [parents] can be the single most important motivating factor in [their] child's life." They go on to say that "sustained effort over time is the key to achievement," and that "perseverance pays off." They also emphasize the importance of being a "good role model," and that "parents can help children see the value of embracing challenges, setting high goals and working hard to achieve them." And lastly, they suggest that parents "hold *realistic* expectations. Holding *high* standards doesn't mean holding *impossible* standards."

Things may also change for parents and their children as far as being as involved as you maybe were when your child was in elementary school. This stage is not as "hands on" as the elementary stage when you were baking cupcakes and volunteering to read a book during story hour. There is a certain emotional distancing that happens when they enter middle school, but there are also new adults in your child's life and many more of them than in the past. Being involved with your child's school doesn't need to end; it may simply need to happen in a different way. According to Lisa Hayes, author of *Growing Pains: The middle school years*, "Often times parents back away when they see their child's thrust for independence. As a result, parent involvement in the middle grades decreases," but, she says, "this is a mistake-middle school kids need you more than ever." Hayes continues to explain that, "It may feel harder to get involved at school when your child has four or five teachers, and each teacher sees around 100 kids each day. As a result, parents may rely on their children when it comes to getting information about the school." Since getting middleschoolers to talk can be "like pulling teeth," Hayes offers some questions, which may help parents more effectively acquire information from their kids.

First of all, parents in general usually learn early on in the game to avoid questions which seek a 'yes or no' answer for the obvious reason. Kids will most often give us only what we ask for, no more and no less, and with no one is this more true than the teenager. Hayes suggests that it is also a good idea to ask a variety of questions ranging from academic to general opinion.

These are some of the questions that parents can ask that will "encourage your kids to fill you in:

Academics:	What do you do best at school? How hard is the work? Do any classes seem difficult?
School Staff:	Which classes do you enjoy the most? Why? Do you feel close to any staff member.
Discipline:	Do people usually follow the school rules? What happens when a rule is broken? Do you have concerns about any of the rules?

Safety:	Do you feel safe at school? If you didn't, would you feel comfortable speaking up?
General opinion:	What do you like best about your school? What would you like to change about your school? What would you tell a friend from another school about your school?"

There are many ways to stay involved at the middle school level such as volunteering to chaperone field trips, helping kids organize bake-sales in order to fundraise for events, or going in to speak about your career or a topic of teen interest. On the part of the school, Hayes says that, "schools should do their best to ease the transition from elementary school to middle school," and that, "schools can help your child adjust to his changing lifestyle more smoothly if they: create ways to decrease the breaking up of the day, provide parents with strategies to support the success of their middle-grade students, and make available educational opportunities geared·to the special interests of middle-grade families." Lastly, Hayes reminds us that, "Even as they're pushing parents away as part of the normal growing pains of adolescence, middle school aged children really want and need their parents to be involved in their lives, especially in school."

2

The Importance of Character Education in Enhancing Adolescent Life Skills

"Intelligence plus character-that is the goal of true education"

—Martin Luther King Jr. (1947)

One principal, of a small New England Public Elementary/Middle School (grades K-8), feels that the middle school age group is by far the most at risk population of children today, as most research would also support. What makes her perspective valuable, is that since she has students from kindergarten through the eighth grade in one building (total student population approximately 140), she is able to witness this shift in dynamics first hand.

New England Principal also stated that her school believes in educating the whole child and began a social skills education program through a grant from one of the state universities. She believes that "a social skills curriculum taught in isolation by a guidance counselor is not only difficult, but very ineffective." Her hope is "by practicing these skills in a more 'real life' setting such as the classroom, that the students will actually develop social skills that will help them throughout their lives." Rushworth Kidder, in *Talking About Ethics and Character Education*, supports this view, and states that character education must "be embedded." He warns educators not to "do a character education program off by itself; don't create an ethics ghetto over in one corner of the curriculum. Instead, he explains, "Integrate it throughout the curriculum." He suggests that educators "develop a conceptual framework, a way to talk about ethics," and to "do more than bring kids together to talk about moral ideas...There is a coherent way to think about the meaning of ethics and to help students wrap themselves around it."

In the younger grades, the students are taught how to properly introduce themselves and greet people, and to supplement these basic skills, New England Principal says that they started a character education program, where positive character traits are acknowledged and rewarded. This program is implemented from kindergarten through the eighth grade, where teachers discuss and practice these positive traits within the classroom. After the end of each quarterly marking period, the students vote on which student they feel most exemplified the designated trait for that marking period. The students are also asked to include a brief comment or example of why they feel this student deserves the award. The teachers gather the information, and together with their own input decide who is the best candidate for the character award. There is an assembly held at the end of each marking period where the awards are presented along with the academic awards. In addition, the teachers of grades K-4 teach something called "apology of action" which involves the students role playing a situation in which one student has done something wrong or hurtful to another student. The students learn that a simple "I'm sorry" isn't always enough and practice ways of taking things a "step further, and make amends for the problem or hurt feeling that they caused."

New England Principal states that this process carries over into the middle school grades when conflicts happen in the hallways, on the soccer field, or between boyfriends and girlfriends. After the conflict has been "dealt with" all parties involved are encouraged "to move on." New England Principal admits that not only is this a good life skill to practice, but also necessary within her school community as "it is so small. It's like a family in that we have to get over things and move on in order to function smoothly."

B. David Brooks and Mark E. Kann, authors of *What Makes Character Education Work*, state that there needs to be certain key elements present for a character education program to be effective. First, there needs to be "direct instruction. Schools cannot assume that language, concepts, behaviors, and skills of good character are written into the genetic code; learned at home, from television, or in the neighborhood; or absorbed through the invisible hand of the general curriculum. Like arithmetic, the teaching of character values such as "responsibility" and "respect" must be purposeful and direct. Students should hear and see the words, learn their meanings, identify appropriate behaviors, and practice and apply the values." Another essential ingredient of a solid character education program is a "Language-based curriculum. Children entering the schools today often lack the vocabulary for understanding basic value concepts such as "honesty" and "courage." Even when they can define such values, they often fail to connect them to their own behavior. Successful character education programs focus students' attention on the basic language that expresses core concepts and links the words to explicit behavior." Brooks and Kann further explain that it is important for educators to demonstrate "positive language. Students must know what is expected of them if they are to practice appropriate behavior. Therefore, common negative language such as "Don't be late" or "Don't forget your pencil" should be translated into explicit positive language as in "Be on time" or "Be prepared."

Another important element to successful character education is "content and process. In addition to teaching the content of consensus and civic values, an effective character education curriculum should provide a process for implementing those values when making decisions. As students learn and practice the decision-making process, they develop the skills needed for making ethical choices." Along with content and process, another key element is "visual reinforcement. Character education is in competition with adverse desires, messages, and pressures in our society. The visual presentation of character values is, in effect, an advertising campaign intended to keep the words, concepts, and behaviors learned in class at the forefront of students' attention. Visual displays illustrate and reinforce good character." Lastly, Brooks and Kann explain that, "schools are, essentially, a community of their own. If the whole school community fosters the language, culture and climate of good character, then the students who spend a significant portion of their time there will acquire the words, concepts, behaviors, and skills that contribute to good conduct, ethical decision-making, and a fertile living environment."

In addition to the Character Education Program, this small New England public school has also implemented a Life Skills Training Program which was devised in order to educate and hopefully prevent dangerous risk-taking behavior in students (grades three through eight). New England Principal explains that, "the program develops several skills such as ways of resisting peer pressure and building communication skills," and that "this program is a carry over of the responsive classroom skills taught in the younger grades. It is more practice at a new level."

As far as addressing sexuality, there is the standard sex education in the fifth grade, which informs students about puberty and the changes that will take place. Then, in eighth grade the more detailed information is presented as far as STD's, pregnancy prevention, and AIDs. In addition, there is a discussion that addresses the emotional element of a sexual relationship, and the students are taught what defines a "healthy" relationship as well as the symptoms of a relationship that is "unhealthy". They often have a panel of teenage guest speakers to discuss relationships and answer any questions that the students may have, including teenage mothers. New England Principal states that it is important "that students understand that unhealthy relationships are often cyclical, and they often do not know or understand the difference between a healthy and an unhealthy relationship."

In addition, New England Principal says that "it is also very important for us as educators, to drive home the point to our students that 4 out of 10 people who go on to abuse alcohol and other drugs later on, started at a very young age." In fact, the program is in the process of inviting a panel of teen alcoholics and addicts to visit with the middle school. This Principal continues to say, "that as much as we drive home the 4 out of 10 statistic, that we also try to focus on the fact that 6 out of 10 *don't* abuse alcohol and other drugs, and that 8 out of 10 *do not* smoke. We make sure that they understand that these seemingly 'harmless to try' drugs, including cigarettes, are the gateway drugs for others down the road."

3

Middleschoolers and Sexuality

"Children must be taught sexual ethics and responsibility, inside and outside the home, just as they are taught how to behave in any number of public and private arenas. Teaching children to have self-respect, to feel good about themselves, to make good decisions: to me, that is sexuality education."

—Dr. Joycelyn M. Elders
author of foreword

Harmful to Minors-the perils of protecting children from sex

—by Judith Levine

Along with the educational, social, and emotional changes that your preteen is going through are the sexual changes that accompany early adolescence. Hormones are flying around recklessly and without direction, changing their orbit and speed at any given moment. For girls, this means that they may have moments of being irritable, or actually being *mean* to someone that they know is a good friend and that they really care about. When the hormonal wave is over, they often feel badly about themselves and wonder what possessed them to say such a thing, especially since they did not mean to say it. It is a mild form of menopause, only in the reverse, and without the *veteran ability* to recognize its arrival, nor the ability to manage it. Instead of hormones slowing down towards the end of a reproductive life stage, they are just getting started, but with the same type of irregularity. Most schools and families now educate children on the early changes of adolescence, but many times the emotional implications of hormonal surges are left out. At least if young girls are made aware of these potentially *nasty* waves, they will be better able to understand themselves and their behavior, and not feel that something is wrong with them, or that it is a newly developing defect of their character. As they become more experienced at being a teen, and more familiar with their body's chemistry, they may even develop the ability to *ride the wave.*

For both boys and girls, hormones also cause them to "get excited" around the opposite gender. Now, when seventh and eighth graders slow dance they may begin to feel a little tingle inside. Girls, when they head off to the bathroom with the rest of the herd to discuss the news of the evening thus far, may notice a little wet spot in their undies. For boys, this tingle feeling may be a little more obvious if he gets an erection, causing him to back up from his slow dance partner and untuck his shirt to prevent embarrassment. Hopefully, these changes have been explained so that these middleschoolers are not wondering whether what they are going through is normal. It is important that they do not feel that they are *different.*

It is also within the normal range of behavior for your early adolescent child to be sneaking peaks at nudie pictures. This can be anything from a Victoria's Secret catalog to a more pornographic magazine from the corner drug store. They are curious about sex and what it means to be sexual. What is important here, is how the parent responds to finding the magazine under the mattress and that they take advantage of a very *teachable moment.* As a woman, I am obviously not thrilled about the exploitation of women (not that exploiting men is all right either), but I am very ready for the inevitable moment to happen with my two sons who are ten and almost fourteen, to explain to them that it is very normal and natural to be curious about these magazines. We will, however, continue our conversation about how these women (or men if it is my daughters) are being portrayed and objectified.

It is also normal for middleschoolers to begin to seek out and explore their pleasure points. Both boys and girls will begin to feel urges to masturbate, and simultaneously will be wondering if everybody else is doing this, too. This can feel shameful, as *guessing* what everybody else is doing and *knowing* what every body else is doing are two different things. In fact, it has been suggested that 99% of males (teens through adults) masturbate and the other one percent is lying. The statistic isn't quite as high for girls, but most teenage girls and women masturbate also. It is a good idea to talk with teens before they enter this stage so that these feelings of shame are prevented, and that they are encouraged to develop and continue to have a healthy relationship with their bodies. Teens are walking around like exposed nerves, hyper-aware of their surroundings, and of every word and nonverbal cue sent their way. Therefore, how we respond to their behaviors and questions is key to the healthy development of our teenage children.

Hopefully, your middleschooler has also had some sex education in school and has been made aware of the potential dangers of engaging in sexual activity before he or she is ready. Most schools teach about pregnancy prevention, STDs and AIDS. Now is a good time, however, to have a follow-up conversation with your very curious middleschooler about the emotional piece that *should* go along with the physical if it is going to be a healthy relationship. Children need to be *taught* emotional responsibility and respect. They need to be taught to think of how a certain behavior or sexual activity may affect the other person. They need to be taught that boys and girls think very differently and they need to be told *clearly* that "No means no." This is the perfect time to convey this ultra-important message.

Now is also a good time to explain about oral sex to your teen. This may be an uncomfortable topic of conversation, but given the oral sex epidemic going on in this country at the present time (which is beginning at younger and younger ages), now would be a good time to have the talk with your teen. This topic will be addressed in later chapters, but for now it is simply important for parents to realize that more than likely their preteen or teen is well aware of what oral sex is, and that they would benefit from some clarification. Mainly, teens need to realize that oral sex *is* sex. They often think that since they cannot get pregnant that it does not count. It counts and they need to hear this from their parents.

4

Middleschoolers, Anger, and Conflict Resolution

Most everyone with teenagers will admit that though there are occasional spontaneous teachable moments throughout adolescence, that the real window of opportunity lies with the preteens. In other words, we are more apt to actually be *heard* during the quiet before the storm. There is still a lingering sense that Mom and Dad are knowledgeable, at least about most things, and the implicit trust that children have in their parents is still alive and well.

Most of us would agree that when we look back and reflect on our own middle school years, that they were some of the hardest we experienced. There are new pressures to fit in and be accepted. There are fears present about not fitting in and not being accepted. There are bullies. Boys get pushed around physically which is humiliating for them, their budding male egos shattered before all who witness it. Girls can get pushed around physically also, but have more of a tendency to do their bullying in more covert, backstabbing ways. They will usually drop someone from the in-crowd for no good reason and with no notice, just to be mean and gain the approval and comradery of those still remaining. They will talk behind her back. They will spread malicious rumors. They will comment on her clothes and hair and laugh in front of everyone.

With hormonal changes and social/growing up changes, conflicts arise, and since their lives will most likely never be completely free of conflict, now is a good time to teach your preteen some strategies to deal with life when it is difficult. They will have to deal with the anger and possibly aggression of their peers. They may be angry themselves. They may even have angry or frustrating moments and not know why. They may just feel all charged up. What happens when teens have these feelings and they are not taught the skills to handle them, the anger or the frustration will leak out sideways. A younger sibling could borrow a pencil without asking and things could start flying (literally). Of course, this will happen to a certain degree anyway, as the nature of a teen is to be egocentric. However, teaching them some basic skills to handle anger and frustration could significantly reduce these moments. It will also limit the negative they will receive from acting out or speaking impulsively and inappropriately.

James Windell, author of *6 Steps to an Emotionally Intelligent Teenager*, writes that, "There seems little question that the behavior of parents shapes the caring feelings and attitudes of children. According to the research psychologists Nancy Eisenberg and Richard Fabes, parents who provide clear messages about the consequences for others of hurtful behaviors tend to have more empathetic children. And parents who discuss emotions with children seem to have children with greater skills of sympathy and empathy." This, of course, goes back to our need to continue role modeling for our children. They will imitate what we do far more than what we say. A parent who smokes and tells their child not to smoke is ineffective and their child will have a significantly higher chance of becoming a smoker than a child of a parent who does not smoke. The "do as I say and not as I do" theory ceases to work at this stage because they are too smart. Not only that, but this may also trigger anger in your preteen and definitely in your teen, as teens tend to actually enjoy focusing on hypocrisy.

Role modeling conflict resolution within the home is extremely important. It is important to try to help your teen see the other perspective as much as he or she will probably resist it. Even if they get out of the conversation that there actually *is* another perspective, then consider your talk a small victory. For teens, it is all about them and it is very difficult to drag them out of *victim mode* once they have slid into it. They will often say that a teacher or a coach "just does not like me," and that he or she is "out to get me, and it is like so obvious. Ask any of my friends." What can be done with these types of situations as well as the vast amount of other teen conflicts, is to teach them to be a little more *cerebral*. This is not natural as teens are walking ids, pleasure points fueled by feeling. However, if you can get the very point across that they can step back and breathe before they react about a situation, some potentially painful experiences may be prevented. What you are teaching them is to take a teen time out, whether it means asking for a pass to go to the bathroom during school just to grab 5 minutes to sort things out, or spending a little time alone after school. You can also explain that this is also a good tool for grown-ups, as most of us are unable to present our best selves when we are over-stimulated with emotion. In fact, I came up with my own acronym that I used throughout the years of working with adolescents and their families. The acronym is S.T.A.R. that stands for Stop, Think, Assess, React. It works well.

By far, the most important strategy to use with your teen is to do your very best to be an *active listener*. Teens can sense, as can anyone else, when they are being tuned out. They will also get annoyed and frustrated, as would anyone else if they are cut off in mid-sentence and prevented from saying what they need to say. Teens also have a very strong need during this life stage to feel empowered, and the best way to do this is to *listen* to them, even if the subject is that your teen wants to dye his hair purple and get a nose ring on the way to a co-ed hot tub party. In your world, where there is only one moon in the sky at night, this may have absolutely no chance of happening; however, simply hearing him out will most likely defuse the bomb somewhat.

Of course one of the primary emotions present during adolescence is anger. When it is expressed outwardly, the teen lands herself in trouble and is forced to deal with the consequences and when she turns it inward, she becomes depressed. It is especially important to teach teens some cerebral skills to handle their anger a little more gracefully. Windell talks about teaching your teen to learn to acknowledge what situations or people tick him off, his anger triggers, and says that, "Helping your child identify some of his personal triggers and helping him recognize how he reacts to them is important. It's an initial step in using his mind to get better control of his emotion." Once she becomes aware of what ticks her off, hopefully together you can come up with a way to minimize her exposure to what triggers her. This is also a good time to explain to him that thoughts precede feelings, therefore as he thinks so he will feel also. Thought control is difficult for most grown-ups, but just like anything else with practice it is a skill that can be mastered. Without angry thoughts, one cannot feel angry.

PART II

Adolescence and Gender Issues in Today's World

5

Boys to Men

✦

What it means to be male in Today's society and how they get there...

Explicit sex in the movies, in videos, and on CDs and tapes has become literally unavoidable. In every urban area huge billboards show men in underwear striking poses that blatantly suggest sex. Women clad in their underwear float by on the sides of buses and cause barely an eyebrow to raise. Sex is used to sell everything to everyone, including to young people. This change in how and what children learn about sex has been so sudden and so dramatic that it's hard for any of us to understand what it means for our

children's sense of themselves. One thing is for sure: boys have always been
particularly avid consumers of whatever sexual information is available.

—Geoffrey Canada
author of *Reaching Up for Manhood*

There has been a good deal of discussion lately about the premature sexualizing of girls via the media and the clothing industry; however, not much has been said about how boys are taking all of this in and what they are doing with their newly acquired information. Sixth-grade boys (and younger of course) are witnessing girls their own age drawing attention to themselves by wearing halter tops that say "sweet thing" and "hot babe." We are beginning to worry about the affect this is having on our young girls, but what about our boys. What is going through their minds when a girl is trying to get a reaction from them that they may not feel ready or able to give? We also have the unfortunate assumption that has been drilled into our boys' heads since the beginning of time which is that part of being a man means to have sex, lots of sex. They are supposed to be thinking about it, talking about it, and trying their best to get it. So what happens to the preteen or teen boy who is at a dance with his friends, surrounded by scantily clad members of the opposite gender and he doesn't feel ready or care yet about any of it?

Readiness to be give and receive sexual attention has much to do with the pituitary gland and genetics, as hormonal chemistry is what kicks all of these feelings in and the timing of hormonal release has everything to do with heredity. As most of us are aware, sexuality is a continuum that begins at birth and evolves through the course of one's development, not something that happens overnight. Little boys and girls realize where their pleasure points are rather quickly as anyone who has had toddlers can attest to. It's not much longer before they become aware of physical differences and become cognizant of being a boy or a girl. They become aware of differences in roles and behavior and of how they are treated because of their genders. As teenagers, they not only become more aware of these differences, but actually become hypersensitive to their newly discovered *maleness* or *femaleness*, as confusing as it all is. They focus on their bodies, the bodies of their peers, and the bodies they see in magazines and on TV. Males and females spend a large part of their days comparing themselves to those around them, both real and imagined.

For young boys, much of what they see on TV and in the movies is the hyper-masculine body driven by high-octane testosterone. They are seeing bulky men whose primary way of resolving conflicts is with the use of violence. No where is this more true than on the set of WWF and RAW, where young males view physically strong, muscle-bound men parading around a wrestling mat threatening their opponent and anyone else who dares to approach them. Most of us are aware, at least let's hope so, that the wrestling shows are choreographed, but to our young male viewers, this does not matter. They are taking in and processing visual pictures that will remain with them forever. They are seeing chairs being smashed over an opponent's head. They are hearing violent language used to dominate and intimidate, and these behaviors are being reinforced by the applause and roar of the WWF and RAW audiences.

To make matters worse, these young boys are viewing these angry acting, powerful men dominating and intimidating women, thereby mixing sexuality and violence, the obvious formula for rape. In fact, when I was first gathering information to write this book, I viewed some old WWF and RAW episodes. It was very difficult to watch at all; however, I must say that my stomach did a back flip when I saw the wrestlers force a woman to drop to her knees and to bark like a dog. He then proceeded to demean her and *punish* her for being disrespectful to him. It terrifies me to think about the long term affects of this TV show on our boys and young men, as well as how it will later affect how they treat women.

Not only does the media support and encourage violence and sexual violence, but it has also affected the way boys and young men perceive their own bodies. What used to be considered a female obsession is rapidly working its way into the young male psyche as well. Both boys and girls question whether they are thin enough, toned up enough, tall enough, and developed enough. Girls worry about their breasts being big enough and their butts being small enough. Boys worry about their penises being big enough, their muscle size, and having a six-pack across their abdomens. They compare, compare, and compare everyday. They watch who has whom for a boyfriend or girlfriend and wonder what it was that attracted them to each other. Teens become hypersensitive to what it means to be physically desirable to the opposite, or in some cases, the same gender. *Desirability*, of course, is directly related to how one perceives one's body regardless of whether this perception is accurate or not. For teens as well as adults, our perception is our reality.

Harrison G. Pope, Jr., M.D., Katharine A. Phillips, M.D., and Roberto Olivardia, Ph.D., authors of *The Adonis Complex* state that, " There's a widespread crisis among today's boys and men-a crisis that few people have noticed. Men of all ages, in unprecedented numbers, are preoccupied with the appearance of their bodies. They almost never talk about the problem, because in our society, men have been taught that they aren't supposed to be hung up about how they look.

But beneath the tranquil surface, we see signs of this crisis everywhere. Millions of men are sacrificing important things in their lives to exercise compulsively at the gym, hoping for a bigger chest or a flatter stomach. Men and young boys alike are buying billions of dollars worth of 'muscle-building' food supplements and diet aids. As many as three million men have taken anabolic steroids or other dangerous black-market drugs to buff up their bodies. An equally large, even more secret group of men has developed eating disorders-compulsive binge eating, dieting, and exercise rituals-that even their girfriends or wives may not know about. Another million or more men have developed 'body dysmorphic disorder, an excessive preoccupation with perceived flaws in their appearance. They worry, for example, that their hair is thinning, their breasts are fat, or their penis is too small. Each year, hundreds of thousands of men seek out cosmetic surgery, from hair implants to liposuction. They've spent billions of dollars on products to smooth their skin or otherwise improve their appearance. Unlike healthy men and boys, they have an unrealistic view of how they look-and so they abuse drugs, exercise excessively, and spend billions on products that are often worthless."

Of course, for the most part, we have the media to thank for this. Our boys and young men are watching TV and movies where hard-bodied actors have women falling all over them. They are seeing pictures in magazines of the *perfect* male body being exemplified by bulky muscles and ripples across the abdomen-now labeled a six-pack. There are no subtitles or captions beneath these photos explaining that to achieve a body like this without the use of steroids is *completely impossible.* They are being led to believe that if they stack enough wood and do enough push-ups that they too can look like this. They are being set up to strive for a goal that is unattainable. Therefore, our boys and young men are being set up to fail before they even begin.

Pope, Phillips, and Olivardia further discuss boys and body image and add that, "As part of this trend to better understand the feelings of contemporary boys, researchers have asked elementary and high school boys whether they like how they look, how they'd prefer to look, what their eating habits are like, and other habits about body image." They found that "many boys are indeed self-conscious about their bodies and unhappy with how they look. One study found that boys are even more dissatisfied with their weight than girls were." The authors continue to discuss a study preformed by Dan Moore where, "895 boys filled out a questionnaire that asked about attitudes toward body image. A surprising 42 percent said that they were dissatisfied with their weight, and 33 percent were dissatisfied with their body shape. Nearly one-third of normal-weight boys were dissatisfied with their weight, and more than two-thirds of those thought they were underweight. But they didn't want to get fatter. Instead, they were most likely to desire a bigger chest and arms and a smaller stomach. In other words, just like many adult men, and just like the boys in our sports camp study, they aspired to the lean and muscular look of GI Joe, Duke Nukem, Batman, or the many similar images in the modern media."

Before we continue to discuss further the issues of our young males, or the following chapter that discusses the issues of our young females, I would like to make it clear that in no way is this a competition between the issues of boys and the issues of girls. In my opinion, both girls and young women and boys and young men in this country are in crisis and in desperate need of emotional connection and guidance. They have been inundated with messages and mixed signals as far as what they are supposed to think and feel and how they are supposed to be. Young boys especially, are very confused about what it means to be male in today's world. They are feeling very locked in to these preconceived stereotypes as far as what they are supposed to think and feel and of what it means to be male in general. The very idea of manhood has been so distorted by the media that they need *healthy manhood* to be redefined for them if they are going to become happy, healthy men. They need redefinition and they need *permission*. These young boys need permission to break free from these expectations and gender stereotypes and to be themselves. They need permission to step outside of the gender box and to just be who they are meant to be.

Until we can get to this point, anger will continue to be a central problem in American culture. As most of us are aware, anger results in two things, violence and depression. Nearly half the world is comprised of males and many of them are angry. We are reminded of this every time we turn on the news, read a newspaper or magazine, or hear of the overcrowding situation in our nation's prisons. Anger has been and continues to be a large problem in this country. Of course, the fabricated male heroes of Hollywood, running on high octane testosterone are much to blame as our young boys try very hard to emulate what they see and view as their male role models and heroes. Bridget Murray writes in *Boys to Men: emotional miseducation* that, "Media images have become more hypermasculine-emotionless killing machines, such as Sylvester Stallone, and have supplanted strong yet milder heroes like Roy Rogers. Many boys learn to hide behind a "mask of bravado." She further states that, "Boys are often victims of ruthless jeering and insults. Many find that words don't stop the taunting but punches do, because anger is the only emotion that earns them respect." Our young males are being saturated with unhealthy messages that repeatedly demonstrate that bigger is better, that might is right and that problems should be solved physically. Rambo and Hulk Hogan don't talk things out and they certainly don't cry.

Thirty years ago we were not hearing of six-year-olds bringing weapons to school or teenagers going on shooting sprees, leaving behind a trail of cold blood and devastated parents and siblings. We are not seeing groups of boys gathering on street corners to talk about feelings of sadness. Instead, the groups of boys gathering on street corners are wearing the same color and gaining acceptance into gangs via *brave* acts of violence. The majority of kids and young adults committing these acts of violence are male and there is a reason. Anger is the one emotion that boys can express that will bring them respect. Anger is viewed as strong and powerful. Sad is viewed as weak and vulnerable.

Anger, when expressed outwardly, brings violence and external conflict. When that same anger is turned inward it causes depression, and never have we seen more depressed young males than we have recently. There are more boys and young men than ever giving up hope, as suicide rates have never been higher. Much of the reason for this is that the symptoms normally noticed and used to treat depression are different for young boys, and they are slipping through the cracks at a rate that now has them in first place as the group most at risk for suicide. William Pollack, Ph.D., author of *Real Boys*, says, "Because society trains boys to cover their sadness, it becomes very difficult for others to know when a boy is not doing well emotionally. Add to it the fact that we generally do not *expect* boys to be sad or depressed-and the fact that if we do suspect depression in boys, *we often use inappropriate methods of diagnosis originally designed to ascertain depression in adult women*-and it should not be surprising that we frequently have a hard time realizing when our sons are unhappy, and often fail to detect (or to accept) depression when it occurs in young and adolescent boys."

Pollack further explains that, "Depression affects boys in a variety of ways. It may make them feel sad, anxious or numb. The depressed boy may act sullen and withdrawn or…may become agitated, overly aggressive, and full of rage. He may misbehave in school or become dependent on drugs or alcohol. Or he may just seem glum. Depression in boys is a syndrome involving a whole range of behavioral difficulties and symptoms. While just about any adult who's been diagnosed with clinical depression will tell you that the experience is quite different from a 'bad mood,' it's essential, especially in the case of boys, to see depression as a kind of wide-ranging syndrome with symptoms that fall along a continuum from mild to extreme. I believe that if we dwell merely on the most extreme-and obvious-instances of full-blown, or 'clinical,' depression, we risk failing to help boys cope with emotional states that, though less intense on the surface, are actually very painful for them, emotional states that without appropriate intervention may very well evolve into a major depression or provoke suicidal feelings."And, Pollack continues, "Bearing in mind too that every depressed boy is likely to have symptoms that look different from those of the next boy, I would recommend that we diagnose depression by watching carefully for the following symptoms:

1. Increased withdrawal from relationships and problems in friendships.

2. Depleted or impulsive mood.

3. Increase in intensity or frequency of angry outbursts.

4. Denial of pain.

5. Increasingly rigid demands for autonomy or acting out.

6. Concentration, sleep, eating, or weight disorders, or other physical symptoms.

7. Inability to cry.

8. Low self-esteem and harsh self-criticism.

9. Academic difficulties.

10. Overinvolvement with academic work or sports.

11. Increased aggressiveness.

12. Increased silliness.

13. Avoiding the help of others.

14. New or renewed interest in alcohol or drugs.

15. Shift in the interest level of sexual encounters.

16. Increased risk-taking behavior.

17. Discussion of death, dying, or suicide.

No matter how healthy a boy's emotional state was when he started life, it quickly becomes compromised by the hardening he feels necessary to avoid feelings of shame, and by his denial (because of shame) of vulnerable emotional states such as sadness, disappointment, and despair. Every boy needs to cry sometimes, to seek the comfort of loving arms, to tell someone how much he hurts and to have them respond with empathy. Yet because of the gender straightjacket that inhibits boys from ever completely experiencing these feelings (let alone expressing them) and insists that they don't need help, boys actively repress feelings of sadness in an unhealthy way that can lead them to feel lonely and frightened, or push them toward more severe forms of depression."

Now, with all of this said about the state or our boys and young men, setting aside the desire to go and hide beneath a big rock, we ask our selves as parents what we can do as far as making some lasting changes to liberate these kids from gender-jail. Well, to begin with, as parents, we need to make a conscious choice to live more deliberately and listen more actively. We need to make an effort to be more aware of the subconscious programming within us that causes the rigidity of gender roles to continue. Passive thinking leads to passive living, and like second-hand smoke, affects everyone around us. What we need to do is to try to catch ourselves in the act, per say, when we are asking our sons for the fifth time in a row to bring the groceries in from the car, or to stack the firewood alongside the garage when we have capable daughters in the house. It means to ask our sons to pick out a recipe that they might like to try and let them pick a night to make dinner for the family. It means to not only *allow* a boy to cry, but *to praise him for it*. We need to teach him that crying is a very healthy way to *get the sad out*. Crying is healing for the spirit. We need to hug and kiss our sons and to tell them that we love them everyday. We also need to reassure them that they do not need to *outgrow* the need for our love and affection. We can wrap our arms around teenagers and young men, too.

This last thought is an important one as boys are very socialized to cut loose emotionally from their parents, especially from their mothers, once they reach early adolescence. This forced separation is also one of the primary causes of boyhood depression and often sends them into an emotional and confusing tailspin. Not only is the loss overwhelming, but they are also left feeling defective, as they question what is wrong with them that they still feel like they need their mom and dad. They wonder what is wrong with them that they miss their mom or dad poking their head in the door to say goodnight. They wonder if they are weird for wanting very normal, healthy affection. To make matters worse, because of the no-talk clause of the boy code, they walk around thinking that they are the only ones that feel this way. It's no wonder that so many of our boys and young men are angry and depressed.

What we can also do to undo some of this, is to educate our young men and women and redefine healthy manhood and womanhood in a classroom setting. Colleges and universities across the country are beginning to add *gender studies* to their curriculums in an attempt not only to eliminate gender straightjackets, but also to shorten the gap between the genders by helping young men and young women to better understand each other. These courses represent the cutting edge of higher education and are being added to curriculums across the country. College students are being taught about physical issues related to their genders, emotional issues involved in sexual relationships, how young men think and interact, how young women think and interact, and much more. Hopefully, in the not too distant future, high school seniors will benefit from gender studies classes in addition to the standard health and sex education classes that are required.

Michael Gurian writes in *Boys and Girls Learn Differently* that, "Sex education is only a piece of the male-female puzzle, and our students know it. They want us to help them know what makes the other tick." He continues, "Sex is one of life's most confusing and crucial activities; it is in no way merely the responsibility of the family. It has never, in fact, been only the family's responsibility. Grandfathers, grandmothers, uncles, aunts, and other people with whom adolescents were bonded have always taught children and adolescents about sexuality. In a school that bonds teachers and students, sex education is a responsible area for discourse and greater wisdom." By teaching our young men and women how each other is wired, we are opening the door for better communication among males and females that can only benefit our society in the future. More than likely, divorce rates would go down in this country, as problems with communication are the number one reason for the dissolution of marriage. If men and women learn to understand each other they will obviously be better able to communicate.

In fact, if we stop to think about what has been taught over the years as far as sex and gender education, it is the natural progression of things. Fifty or sixty years ago there was no sex education. Forty or so years ago, boys and girls were separated and taught the *basics* only. Things were kept very much separate. As things moved along, boys and girls were integrated and taught a little more such as options for birth control and the dangers of sexually transmitted diseases. In the past few years, kids have had character education worked into the standard health class curriculum and are now being taught how to respect each other, resolve problems, and negotiate their way through challenging situations. Both boys and girls are being taught that "no means no." Now, in 2005, the time is right to take things a step further, and to actually teach boys and young men and girls and young women about each other, about their styles of thinking and relating, as well as to help them understand the myths of the boy and girl codes and gender straightjackets. By doing so, our young men and women will learn to be more emotionally available to themselves as well as to each other. This awareness will also carry over into their future relationships, helping them to be better husbands, wives, and partners, as well as better parents.

6

Girls to Women

♦

What it means to be female in today's society and how they get there...

Adolescence is the most formative time in the lives of women.
Girls are making choices that will preserve their true selves or
install false selves. These choices have many implications for
the rest of their lives.

—Mary Pipher, Ph.D
Author of Reviving Ophelia

Though it has been a decade since Mary Pipher, Ph.D. published her best-selling book *Reviving Ophelia*, most of what she had to say then still holds true today, and in some ways even more so. She begins by stating that, "Adolescence in America is the psychological equivalent of toddlerhood. Just as toddlers move away from their parents physically, so adolescents move away from their parents emotionally. There are continuous negotiations between parents and children about distance. Children want to explore and parents want to keep them safe. And both toddlers and adolescents are outraged when their parents don't agree with them about the ideal balance of freedom and security." And, Pipher continues, "Adolescence is currently scripted in a way that builds in conflict between teenagers and their parents. Conflict occurs when parents try to protect daughters who are trying to be independent in ways that are dangerous. Teenagers are under great social pressure to abandon their families, to be accepted by peer culture and to be autonomous individuals."

The teenage girl is developing in many different ways. To begin with, her body is changing. She is beginning to lose her childlike, curve-less physique, as she develops the more shapely appearance of the young woman she is on her way to becoming. She is sprouting breasts and adjusting to wearing a new article of clothing, the training bra. Her hair may become oily. She may get pimples. She may gain weight in the hips and thighs area, especially around the time that she will begin to menstruate for the first time, another huge change for her to deal with. She will have to wear a sanitary pad, and eventually may choose to use tampons, an experience which can be very different at first. Also, these changes are happening at younger ages. It is no longer uncommon for girls as young as nine years old to get their periods for the first time. It would seem that this may be quite a bit for such a young child to handle, when she is still swinging on the swing set and playing with Legos, and now is forced by the laws of biology to become grown-up.

The way she perceives her body, unfortunately, also undergoes a change. The majority of girls become increasingly dissatisfied with how they look, the cognitive predecessor for the eating disorder. According to Kate Fox, author of *Mirror, Mirror-A summary of research findings on body image*, "In one American survey, 81% of ten-year-old girls had already dieted at least once. A recent Swedish study found that 25% of 7 year old girls had dieted to lose weight-they were already suffering from body image distortion, estimating themselves to be larger than they really were. Similar studies in Japan have found that 41% of elementary girls (some as young as 6) thought they were too fat. Even normal-weight and underweight girls want to lose weight."

I do not believe that this is new news for any of us. What is even more unfortunate, however, than the already overwhelming exposure to ultra-thin models and actresses, is that girls are beginning to notice these women at younger and younger ages. And just like anything else, what children see, they emulate. Even when these young girls are running around on the soccer field, the information runs with them, filed away neatly to emerge at a time when something challenges their self-image or their concept of what it means to look attractive. The information may be retrieved while getting ready for a first date or school dance, or possibly it may emerge during late-night *girl talk* over popcorn at a sleep-over party when accumulated messages are shared in confidence. In fact, Fox says that though "the physical changes associated with puberty soon bring [boys] closer to the masculine ideal-i.e. they get taller, broader in the shoulders, more muscular etc...that for girls...puberty only makes things worse. The normal physical changes-increase in weight and body fat, particularly on the hips and thighs, take them further from the cultural idea of unnatural slimness. A Harvard Study showed that up to two-thirds of underweight 12-year-old girls considered themselves to be too fat. By 13, at least 50% of girls are significantly unhappy about their appearance. By 14, focused, specific dissatisfactions intensified, particularly concerning hips and thighs. By 17, only 3 out of 10 girls have not been on a diet-up to 8 out of 10 will be unhappy about what they see in the mirror."

The adolescent girl's perceived body image and level of beauty in relation to her peers also has a lot to do with her social acceptance and is directly related to the age old formation of the clique. This relationship, the connection between what is perceived to be desirable by the middle school or high school populous and the formation of exclusive social groups has not changed. All that has changed are the rules of fashion and body decorating. What used to be skin-tight designer jeans and velour shirts during the 80's, has turned into half-shirts, low-cut jeans which just barely cover the pubic hair line, tattoos, and belly rings. Willingness to conform has everything to do with social acceptance and clique formation during adolescence, especially during the middle school years. Another factor involved in the social grouping of girls, is their susceptibility to the thoughts and opinions of others. Johnson, Roberts, and Worell, say in *Beyond Appearance-a New Look at Adolescent Girls* that, "the tension between the cultural ideal of female beauty and the physical reality of the female body is magnified by two aspects of female gender role expectations. One, female identity is defined in rational terms, and two, beauty is a core aspect of female identity. Girls are expected to be interpersonally oriented, to care about others' feelings, needs, interests, and as a result, girls are more vulnerable than boys to others' opinions of them and behaviors toward them."

Girls care about what people think, especially other girl people. For the most part, the middle school girl will say whatever about whomever in order to be accepted. Most middle schools have several social sub-groups, but there is usually only one *in-crowd*, and the dynamics of these *desirables* can be very interesting and often intense, especially if you are one of those who does not meet up to the group's standards and is cast out on the curbside. It is also possible that the group may randomly choose to cast someone out for no other reason than to be purely mean and cruel. A weak link in the group is often the vehicle for *the Queen* to assert and reaffirm her leadership and power. The following is an excerpt of a confession by a twenty-year old college student taken from *Girlfighting*, by Lyn Mikel Brown,

"It was in fourth grade that I discovered what popularity meant…friends, security, and the envy of my peers…I started to associate myself with the popular girls. I worked my way in slowly, quietly, and took a back seat to the "leaders" of the group. I dressed like they did, walked like they did…It was difficult and it drove my parents crazy, but it was necessary to attain rank.

By fifth grade I was there. I was popular. I made sacrifices along the way, losing touch with my best friend who didn't fit the "mold," using my allowance to supplement the clothes allowance my parents gave me in order to buy designer clothes, spending my winter recesses freezing on the playground because wearing a hat wasn't cool, sleeping over at strangers' houses where I wasn't comfortable because the hostess had popular status, and putting down others to ensure my place at the top.

Talking behind "friends" backs became second nature, and I became an excellent liar to deal with the rare occasions when people confronted me about my inconsistencies…We cut down others because we didn't know how else to ensure that we wouldn't be the ones teased relentlessly. We were selective about who we hung out with so others would feel privileged if we accepted them…

As the leader, I encouraged my friends to find fault in others. I didn't see any other way for us to maintain an image of perfection unless others were imperfect. In this way, I wanted to ensure that I would remain the leader of our group. I'd seen others fall from the throne, finally seen for their conniving and hurtful ways, and I worked over-time to be sure that didn't happen to me.

Within the group, I picked one target to put down, seeing in her the goodness and the ability to reveal to the others the type of person I was. I made her days difficult, finding her sensitive areas and using them as ammunition against her. She was from a home where her mother had a mental illness and her father was an alcoholic, something that I knew was abnormal and easy to justify as faulty. Despite the fact that such things were out of her control, the others followed my lead and teased her as often and as harshly as I did. I was successful; she finally left the group and didn't reappear until the eighth grade when she was ready to confront me."

As would be inevitably expected, the tables turned on her and this now college student recalls that she began to awaken to the fact that,

"My peers despised me; they all wanted to be like me, but they hated me...Everyone treated me with respect, wanted to gain popularity by associating with me, but they were all talking about me behind my back."

When speaking of the elite in-crowd that she once led,

She said that they "came back for me with a vengeance. They were still a powerful force and were able to convince the entire school to hate me. There were notes on my desk when I got to class that read 'DIE BITCH!' and I couldn't get so much as a look from any guys. They ruined me, devastated me to the point of missing nineteen days of school in eighth grade and I felt I deserved every minute of it."

This tale of the rise and fall of an *in-crowd queen,* is unfortunately typical of many middle school social systems. It is also interesting to look at the role that meanness plays in these relationships, primarily those in middle school, as sixth to eighth grade seems to be the peak season for cliques and in-crowd formation. Female aggression is alive and well during these years and actually plays a role in maintaining the hierarchy of the adolescent elite. Johnson, Roberts, and Worrell, write in *Beyond Appearance,* when speaking of research done on a certain clique, spoke of the "complicated phenomena of popularity and isolation." They continue to explain that meanness "was an effective strategy for maintaining popularity for these junior high school girls. Girls who were not super nice or who did not satisfactorily meet an egalitarian norm of niceness risked losing their popularity by being called stuck-up, but girls who transformed the support and power of their popular position into meanness sidestepped such accusations or feelings of envy. Their reputation for meanness acted as a deterrent to both competition *and* suggestions that one was stuck-up. A girl's effectiveness in using meanness to protect her popularity, however, depended on having status in the group. Thus, in a social context in which open competition among girls was unacceptable, meanness became an effective discourse about hierarchical position, popularity, and invulnerability." A similar study done by another researcher found that, "the growing dislike of the popular girls helped them maintain their distance from the unpopular girls and reified their position at the top of the hierarchy."

In discussing the saliency of backstabbing amongst girls, Sharon Lamb, ED.D. writes in *The Secret Lives of Girls* that, "Whether it is too tough to keep up the "good" work because girls long for a bit of the power or respect that outspoken, more aggressive girls command, girls find ways to speak in mean ways without challenging the male-dominated institutions they rely on. In addition, girls have a particular power to wound one another because the cut comes from a supposed ally." She continues to say that, "support for the idea that girls are imitating ways of thinking that male-dominated society produces comes from looking at the ways girls attack each other. Girls don't become mean to each other about what we think of as girl-centered kinds of issues (disloyalty, for example, or caring) but about how appealing a girl looks (how appealing to a boy, that is) or how she is dressed."

Though more covert forms of aggression such as back-stabbing exist within all social classes, they are far more prevalent amongst middle-class girls for the reason that for these girls to express aggression outwardly is considered "wrong and bad. They see it as making them more male and less female. When they are aggressive they have deep, long-lasting feelings of guilt about even the smallest acts of meanness." Lamb continues to explain that "today aggression is permitted among those girls in our society for whom we don't care much, whose development and futures are of little concern. But adults rein in middle-class girls' lives so that the smallest slip of aggression tends to haunt them into adulthood. Society ignores and accepts the aggression in girls from low-income neighborhoods because their images don't matter." In fact, Lamb explains, "because Americans deem aggression in women inappropriate, this expectation keeps low-income women down, in impoverished neighborhoods where it is both accepted and necessary." Of course, to be upset and angry over what others have many would agree to be appropriate and fitting with what would be considered to be human nature. Lamb states that, "Only when aggression takes place in a middle-class setting does it become a cause of concern."

For middle-class girls in particular, Lamb says, "The message that aggression is inappropriate shackles them with feelings of guilt for acts that if performed by male children would be dismissed with a simple "boys will be boys." Research shows that mothers increasingly punish girls for aggression and decreasingly punish boys. American culture further indicts girls for their so-called sneaky aggression, the way they use social exclusion, gossip, and caddiness to punish and hurt." Rarely do people acknowledge or comment on the fact "that girls are not permitted to confront the other person with whom they are mad in a different way."

Something that will be addressed in more detail in a later chapter is some of the other ways that girls can manifest their anger and aggression, specifically, self-mutilation. Therapists are seeing more and more "cutters", girls who cut themselves in order to relieve psychological pain or the reverse, girls who are experiencing a state of detached, psychological numbness who are attempting to feel something. This prolonged condition of emotional detachment serves as a coping mechanism that enables an individual to *leave*, in a sense, a situation that is emotionally unbearable. The most common cases of dissociation usually occur following sexual abuse, where the individual, usually female, mentally *checks out* in order to survive what has happened or what continues to happen to her. The high majority of *cutters* are trauma survivors.

Of course, another route that anger and aggression can take is in the form of the eating disorder, including anorexia, bulimia (the voluntary purging of food already consumed), as well as over-eating. Girls who have been sexually abused will often over-eat, not only because they have become depressed, but as a subconscious attempt to create a *shield* of appearing unattractive and therefore less desirable to potential perpetrators. Girls who are angry, depressed, or anxious often feel the need to take control which would lead them down the path of anorexia. Often, when girls feel out of control or if they come from a stern, authoritarian household, will become anorexic in an attempt to control the only thing they can, what goes into their mouths. Self-punishment plays a strong roll regardless of the avenue they choose for their anger and aggression, as the underlying dynamic is the self-loathing they feel underneath. These feelings are overwhelmingly powerful for the incest survivor and victims of other sexual abuse, as the toxicity of the shame they feel underneath is omnipotent. Punishing themselves via self-harm can be extremely rewarding for these girls. Sometimes, however, eating disorders result from a hyper-focus on body image and comparisons. Girls' failed attempts at dieting may cause them to take drastic measures that can gradually become habitual.

For many girls, it is all about popularity and being accepted, and unfortunately the majority of these social requirements are based on physical appearance, willingness to conform, family socioeconomic status, and to some degree, race.

This translates into the fact that *in-crowds* across the country, for the most part, are made up of white, middle-class kids. Those who do not fit the current mold for beauty, as well as the financial ability to keep up with fashion and the latest teen toys, are often kept outside the circle. Within the world of the female adolescent, this creates a lot of pressure. She has to be thin and have the right clothes. She has to be strong, but not too strong as this can be considered a "turn-off" to boys. She may not need to be rich per say, but she certainly can't come from the "other side of the tracks". Most importantly, she has to be willing to conform to the needs of *the group*. She has to have a willingness to back-stab or at least go along with back-stabbing. To stand up for an *undesirable* could be the equivalent of social suicide. There is a lot of pressure on the adolescent girl to fit in, pressure that most parents dramatically underestimate. For the most part, fitting in is the primary objective and focus of her day. The majority of her energy is tied up with worrying about what is or is not socially acceptable, with much of the emphasis on how she looks. Girls who aren't perceived to be at a certain level of beauty usually do not even make the first cuts for in-crowd acceptance. The adolescent female very much wants to be considered *inside* the circle.

When we speak of adolescent girls fitting in and wanting and needing to be considered inside the circle, we are speaking of a yearning for female solidarity. Especially in the area of athletics, we see very clearly that girls can and do unite in a healthy way. They are able to be supportive and positive towards each other, and to be competitive in a healthy manner. What undermines a very natural ability and desire for girls to pull together are the many underlying and confusing messages they are receiving about what it means to be female and their place as a female in their world. In discussing a plan to achieve female solidarity, Lamb explains that, "Unless proposed solutions to girls' caddiness and exclusivity acknowledge and find more direct ways to honor girls' anger and self-righteousness as well as their very human feeling of competition, rather than covering them over with "good girl" values of caring and sympathy, the girl-to-girl solidarity will have a falseness to it." Lamb continues to say that, "A real solidarity can be built through shared anger. Helping girls to identify common enemies can help, whether they are "the media" or "the system of inequality" or "poverty." If girls fight against these forces together, they can build solidarity while integrating feelings of anger with caring."

As we have explored the relationship between physical appearance and social acceptance, we now need to move on to the teenage girl's awareness of her body in and of itself, especially the changes in shape that her body is undergoing. During this life stage, she is hyper-focused on how she looks. She may spend hours in front of the mirror fussing with her hair to get it to look just right, turning this way and that way in order to get a perspective from various angles of how she is presenting herself to the world. If she likes what she sees in the mirror than all is well with the universe and her day can proceed as scheduled. However, if she does not like what she sees than her mood can quickly plummet into the depths of teenage depression. It doesn't take much and it doesn't take long for her to feel really bad about herself. In fact, the negative internal dialogue that she will rehearse all day long may not even be real. All that it takes to sink a teenage girl is a glance in the mirror at the wrong time, or with a predisposed filter of how she *thinks* she sees herself. This filter often develops after looking at the cover of a teen magazine and noticing slim teenage girls, or a glance in the window of McDonald's after a Big Mac. It is not uncommon for a teenage girl to perceive herself as larger than she was 20 minutes prior to eating lunch.

As there is no one more important in the teenage girl's world but herself, she will interpret nearly every comment within a thirty-mile radius to be about her. If she hears from so and so that Johnny-popular-athlete has a crush on someone, she will more than likely assume that it is her, or the other scenario, that it couldn't possibly be her. Either way, the sun and its planets revolve around her. This very black and white emotional roller coaster that our teenage daughters are on can make it tough to parent them. We may be constantly guessing what it is she is *really* thinking or feeling. We may walk in on her sobbing uncontrollably on her bed with her face buried in her pillow, proclaiming that her world as she had known it has ended, and that she cannot possibly face so and so at school tomorrow. A half an hour later she comes down the stairs for a snack, sits herself down on the couch next to you, and says, "so, what's going on?" Meanwhile, you have marked the yellow pages and made a lengthy list of good adolescent counseling centers in your area. You pinch yourself to make sure this is all real as she seems to be fine. She *is* fine. It feels like you are the one who needs treatment.

Of course there are times when the regular roller coaster ride of adolescence becomes severe enough to warrant professional help (which will be discussed in a later chapter), however, for the most part, some emotional turbulence is to be expected. As teens can rise as quickly as they fall, there will also be occasions when she is thinking that she is the best thing since ice cream on the cone. All it takes is for her to score a few goals in the soccer game, get the highest grade in the class, or get asked on a date by Mr. In-crowd and girlfriend will be flying high in the sky. She will be thinking she is pretty incredible. Not only that, but she will know everything about everything, so if there is anything that you may want to know, go ahead and ask her. She will more than likely be happy to fill you in with her extensive knowledge accumulated over the past 14 years, minus the first five that she does not have a memory of. You may be thinking that now might be a good time to take up meditating as well as figuring out a way to work weekly therapeutic massage into your budget.

Along with *polar feeling* comes *polar thinking*, which actually is in the reverse order since thoughts come first. Your daughter's feelings are black and white and so are her thoughts. So and so is her best friend or she wants nothing to do with her. Of course this could all change tomorrow so don't cross her off the Christmas card list just yet. She may be completely into soccer or softball, and then all of the sudden lose interest entirely. As far as world issues, you can be sure that she has an opinion, and the right one. She has the facts all mapped out in her head so there is certainly no need for her to waste her valuable life space listening to anybody else. They probably wouldn't know a whole lot anyway. Your teenage daughter will see pretty much anything as a complete waste of her time, especially family outings.

If you have brought your daughter up in a certain religion, and to believe certain things, there is a good chance that these beliefs may be challenged. She may even take a temporary leave of absence, but more that likely will be back after the storm passes and the debris clears. Of course, the worst thing a parent can do at these moments is enter into a power struggle. Teenagers thrive on power struggles. The more you push, the more they will push back, and they will enjoy every minute of it. They perceive being forced to get in the car to attend church or to believe in a certain way as a threat to the autonomy they are so desperately striving for. Be assured that they will rise to the challenge with sword and shield in hand. The bottom line is that what will work best in the big picture is to choose your battles. Consciously decide what you need to stand firm on no matter what, and what areas maybe aren't as important where you can either compromise or let go of them completely. Obviously anything that would affect the teen's safety such as rules about who they are allowed in the car with, where they are allowed to be or not allowed to be, phone calls home if plans change, etc., should never be compromised. Letting go of the smaller issues, especially what her beliefs *should be*, however, is a good idea and will empower your newly budding young adult.

As far as the development of the teenage girl's academic self, Pipher says that, "Schools have always treated girls and boys differently." She continues to explain that, "In classes, boys are twice as likely to be seen as role models, five times as likely to receive teachers' attention and twelve times as likely to speak up in class. In textbooks, one-seventh of all illustrations of children are girls. Teachers chose many more classroom activities that appeal to boys than to girls. Girls are exposed to almost three times as many boy-centered stories than girl centered stories. Boys tend to be portrayed as clever, brave, creative, and resourceful, while girls are depicted as kind, dependent, and docile. Girls read six times as many biographies of males than females. Even in animal stories, the animals are twice as likely to be males." As far as these gender related differences in teaching styles and curriculum, Patricia Phelan, Ann Locke Davidson, and Hanh Cao Yu say in *Adolescent Worlds-negotiating family, peers, and school*, that, "When the school as an institution, or the people in it, promote roles, aspirations, or estimates of worth to girls that differ from those it offers to boys, gender borders exist. Gender borders can be found in both the substance and the process of the educational experience-in the content of the curriculum (i.e., when the history and accomplishments of one group are fully or partially excluded), in pedagogical styles and methods (i.e., when teacher attention and encouragement are more frequently directed toward one gender group), and in attitudes and expectations (i.e., when the sensibilities, problems, and assets of one gender group are viewed differently from those of another). Gender borders not only undermine self-confidence and block students' perceptions of what is possible for themselves and others, but also discourage or impede the acquisition of skills necessary to pursue specific careers."

Peggy Orenstein, author of *School Girls*, says that research reported by the AAUW survey, "discovered that the most dramatic gender gap in self-esteem is centered in the area of competence. Boys are more likely than girls to say that they are "pretty good at a lot of things" and are twice as likely to name their talents as the thing they like most about themselves. Girls, meanwhile cite an aspect of their physical appearance. Unsurprisingly, then, teenage girls are much more likely than boys to say that they are "not smart enough" or "not good enough" to achieve their dreams." Orenstein continues to say that, "The educational system is supposed to provide our young people with opportunity, to encourage their intellectual growth and prepare them as citizens. Yet students in the AAUW survey reported gender bias in the classroom-and illustrated its effects-with the canniness of investigative reporters. Both boys and girls believed that teachers encouraged more assertive behavior in boys, and that, overall, boys receive the majority of their teachers' attention. The result is that boys will speak out more readily..."

As most of us are aware, these in-coming messages both subtle and not so subtle, become subconscious. Girls are taking all of this in and filing it neatly in their minds for a later date when it may be useful. Even young girls become aware and responsive to what they perceive is the expected behavior for their gender. They pick up very early on that they are supposed to be nurturing and caring towards others, and that if they react physically over a conflict that they are being aggressive, whereas a boy is often just being a boy. Though both the boy and the girl may receive the same consequence for hitting or pushing in a school setting, the aggressive behavior does not raise eyebrows as much for the boy as it would for the girl. Boys are expected to be physical whereas girls are not. As far as the overuse of the male pronoun in literature, and reading stories where the majority of the protagonists are male, no matter how subtle it may seem, still exemplifies male dominance. On some level, the message being conveyed to students is that the world is all about boys, and that boys are more important. This is obviously not a good message for either gender to internalize, especially in a school setting where the focus is on learning and building a future.

Things have changed somewhat in 2005, but for the most part, unfortunately, most of this still holds true. In fact very recently, my oldest son was playing with my youngest daughter and one of her stuffed animals. He kept referring to the animal as 'he'. I was of course curious about this and asked him how he knew that this seemingly androgynous stuffed animal was male and my son responded with, "whenever there is no specific gender, you always assume that it is male, just like in school when we read stories and nothing is said about an animal character being a boy or a girl, you always assume it is a boy." This, he did not pick up at home. In fact, even when we go on walks, I will alternate genders when we notice wildlife, saying things such as, " look at that mallard. Isn't he graceful the way he landed on the pond, or look at that fox. Isn't she regal the way she stands there so still…" Since he did not grow up in a home which encourages role genderization, it would appear that my son's comment is a fairly obvious example of how these seemingly subtle cues within literature and everyday lesson plans are still very much present even in 2005.

According to Dianne Rothenburg, author of *Supporting Girls in Early Adolescence*, " The development of a positive self-image is critical in the middle grades. Many educators report a general decline in school performance among girls as they enter adolescence. As a group, for example girls exhibit a general decline in science achievement not observed for boys, and this gender gap may be increasing. And, she continues, "The relationship between a decline in self-concept and a decline in achievement indicates that identifying the special needs of female students at school and at home should be a high priority for parents and teachers." When Rothenburg addresses the reason for the apparent connection between low self-esteem and low academic performance, she says, "Reasons for the decline in self-esteem and the accompanying decline in academic achievement are not clearly indicated by research, but it likely that multiple factors are involved. The

AAUW study found evidence that boys receive preferential treatment in school from teachers. The researchers found that boys ask more questions, are given more detailed and constructive criticism of their work, and are treated more tolerantly than girls during outbursts of temper or resistance. Out-of-school factors probably also play a role: some observers suggest that, as they grow older girls' observations of women's roles in society contribute to their changing opinions about what is expected of girls. If girls observe that women hold positions of less status than men in society, it may lead girls to infer that their role is less important than that of boys or that they are inferior to boys."

Now is also a good opportunity to discuss the importance of the mother-daughter relationship and the importance of role modeling a balanced life. Much has been said about how a daughter's future opposite-gender relationships will have a great deal to do with what her relationship was like with her father. If her father was kind and affectionate, and respected the females in the family, a daughter will most likely pursue someone of the same emotional caliber. Just as Dad has the ability to influence how his daughter will perceive men, so it is also true for moms and what her daughter's perception of motherhood will be like. In this insanely fast-paced society, where mothers are expected to do and be everybody's everything, to burn the candle at both ends, and maintain the status of last on the family list, it is a mother's duty to role model good self care and creating a balanced life. Of course it would probably be easier to lead a guided tour through a Brazilian rain forest, however, this is of utmost importance as the momentum is not in our favor. We have become a society of over-scheduled, over-committed, anxious runners, feeling the need to make productive use of every minute in the day. Many of us are frazzled and stressed out, as we are being fueled by nervous energy, yet we continue to run on empty. We continue to zap frozen dinners in the microwave and plant ourselves in front of the television because we are too drained and exhausted to sit as a family. This is very bad, because the girls of today are going to have quite a job keeping up with the standards of today's moms because we are doing it all and them some. In fact, the feeling would be similar to getting straight A's and being on the honor roll. The next semester there is really no where to go but down. At best, if she maintains the straight A status, then she has merely *met* the standard, and if not, there is a feeling of failure and inadequacy.

When we are running around like anxious gazelles, not only are we betraying ourselves, we are also not being good role models. What our girls need from us, is to witness us taking good care of ourselves, and to see us give ourselves permission to hold off of on cleaning the bathroom, put our feet up, and sit down to read a magazine. Our daughters need to hear us say *no*, and to understand the value of this very important word. When they experience us politely declining people who ask us to take on something that we know is too much and could send us over the edge, they get the message loud and clear that taking care of ourselves is a *good* thing, and a healthy expression of self-love. They will get it that limiting the stress in one's life is healthy for the individual as well as those around her, as for the most part, crabby, stressed out people are not that much fun to be around. It is also good for her to see Mom delegate household tasks, whether Mom works outside the home or not. This is one of the best ways to demonstrate self-respect for your daughter and to prevent "the doormat syndrome", as the obvious message is that it is not Mom's job to be *everybody's everything*. Just as with anything else, we can talk about self-respect, assertiveness, and stress management until we are blue in the face, however, it is what we *do* that matters most. For kids, role-modeling is everything. We have become a generation of *straight A moms*, perpetual honor-rollers, involved in every extracurricular activity and club offered. We are doing it all and more in order to *have* it all and more, but the price we are paying is enormous. What they witness as far as our adult behavior will likely have a large impact on what they value, and how they will treat themselves and others when they grow up.

It is very important for us as parents to realize that there are as many messages being fired through our teenager's atmosphere, as there are rays from the sun. We will most likely not catch all of them, but if we can do the best we can to intercept some of them and to teach her how to process what is out there, then she will be better able to allow her own strengths to shine through. We can teach her to ignore wafer-like women on billboards and in magazines. We can do this by explaining to her about the advertising industry. We can discuss her strengths and support her in areas that she may need to work on. We can teach her to allow herself to be smart and athletic without worrying if her new boyfriend will find her intimidating. With the support, encouragement, and education that her parents can provide she can learn to repel society's messages and to embrace her own unique gifts and her true self, and with full confidence. She can learn to feel good about taking care of herself, and that by doing so, will not only be better able to express love towards others, but she will be more open and able to experience joy in her own life.

7

Gay and Lesbian Young Adults Speak

"As mental-health professionals have long told us, the basic predicament of living like a second-class citizen and actively hiding the truth about ourselves diminishes our personal dignity and our self-esteem-even when we might not be aware of it-and our impaired self-esteem leads to many complex emotional problems."

—Michelangelo Signorile
Author of *Outing Yourself*

I don't think that any of us, when we are gleaming through the nursery window at our newborn infant for the first time think about the conversation we may have someday when he tells us that he is gay. We have dreams for our children, and hope that their lives will be happy, fulfilling, and free of painful experiences. We don't want them to have anything *extra* to deal with whether it be diabetes or

45

a learning disability. We don't want their lives to be hard. Debra W. Haffner, M..P.H., author of *Beyond the Big Talk* states that, "by the time a child comes out to a parent, they have probably had these feelings for years," and that "in general, there was a three-and-a-half-year spread between feeling sexually attracted to someone of the same sex and labeling oneself as gay or lesbian." Haffner continues to explain that, "accepting one's sexual orientation is part of the developmental task of forming a sexual identity," and that according to the American Psychological Association, sexual orientation is "an enduring emotional, romantic, sexual, or affectional attraction to another person…sexual orientation exists along a continuum that ranges from exclusive homosexuality to exclusive heterosexuality and includes various forms of bisexuality." In addition, Haffner states that "Many gay and lesbian adults report that they had an early sense of being different from their peers. About 20 percent recognized that they were gay prior to puberty or just around the time of puberty. Forty percent understood that they were gay in high school, and the other 40 percent self-identified in college."

We also need to know, that if we are *straight* parents, we cannot possibly conceive of what it is like to be in the skin of our gay or lesbian teen. We can guess, but we cannot know. Day in and day out, life is different for them than it is for straight kids. Haffner reminds us that we "need to know that it is tough to be a gay teenager, despite greater societal openness about homosexuality. Gay teens face many problems compared to their heterosexual peers. They are five times more likely to be the targets of violence and harassment, three times more likely to be injured in a fight severely enough to warrant medical treatment, and nearly twice as likely to be threatened or injured by someone with a weapon. Gay teens are two times more likely to use alcohol, three times more likely to use marijuana, and eight times more likely to use cocaine and crack than straight teens. Gay and bisexual teens are (depending on the study) three to seven times more likely to attempt suicide than their heterosexual peers. Many report dismay over same sex attractions, social and emotional isolation, and low self-esteem and abuse not only from peers but also family members."

I had the opportunity to speak with several gay and lesbian young adults about the process by which they came to terms with their sexual orientation, as well as the initial conversations they had with their families. One gay young adult, presently a junior in college, when asked how old he was when he first realized that he was gay responded with, "I always knew." He continued to say that, "I always knew it, and that it was more a matter of accepting it." And, he said, that when people started to talk about liking girls, "that I thought something was wrong with me." This student went to an all boys' Catholic high school where he said he began to realize his sexual orientation during his freshman year, and that by his sophomore year he was starting to tell people that he was gay.

When asked about his most difficult time as a gay teen, he said without hesitation, "middle school. It was like hell on earth." He continued to say, "I don't remember people. I don't remember names. I just remember that there were a lot of people. I had a high pitched voice and I talked a lot with my hands. I guess I had all of the *signs*. I heard a lot of *gay* and *faggot*." This gay student went on to say that his first reaction was to deny it because being gay had such a "negative connotation." He said that he was teased by both boys and girls and that he felt that he was a "target" of this teasing originally because he was just different as far as how he dressed and wore his hair, and that this teasing moved into being teased about being gay, even though he did not even "get it" yet himself that he was gay. He said that some of the kids went on-line and began harassing him via e-mail. In fact, this gay college student said that one of his most painful memories was when these kids who he went to middle school with again found him via computer after he had been away at private high school for two years. He said that there was one kid in particular who was questioning him about being gay, and thinking there was a chance that this kid was sincerely curious and realizing that he did not want to hide anymore, decided to admit his sexual orientation. He said that he was just starting to realize it and thought, "what can happen by just saying yes, I am gay." It wasn't long before he was made aware that printed copies of the e-mail conversation were dispersed among his ex-middle school classmates. He said, "It was really horrendous."

When I asked him how he survived middle school, he answered with, "I never lashed back. I don't even think that I would have been able to as I didn't have much confidence back then. I do remember that I had no desire to change who I was. I found solace with my teachers, and actually befriended some of them which helped me to separate from the kids. I also saw a guidance counselor each week, though I would say that my main defense mechanism was to withdraw." He went on to say that even at this young age that he knew that "these kids were just mean and that I myself had never had any desire to do anything evil to anyone. I couldn't help to think that adults were people that were more like me, more reasonable, more level-headed, and that they weren't going to make fun of me. They were the reason I got through."

He said that the gay bashing was so severe at times and the teasing such torture that he "cried a lot privately at home." There was another instance that involved one of the middle school students trying to set him up with a girl for a date. This gay middle-school student (at the time) decided to take the path of least resistance thinking that it would be easier to go along with it, and agreed to go out with the girl. He was instantly humiliated when the girl laughed at him and he realized that the majority of the school was in on the joke. It had been a well-planned conspiracy to get him to agree to go out with this girl for the sole purpose of publicly mocking him.

Upon graduating middle school he decided that he wanted to be far away from where he had been, and applied to this very reputable all boys' Catholic school, not because it was all male or Catholic, but simply because he wanted "to be someplace else. I just wanted to be away from where I was. I wanted to be someplace where I could survive." He said that, "it was just one of those things that it happened to be Catholic," but that what he wanted was "a blank slate. I just wanted to start over, and this happened to be a really good school." This school ended up being a good choice for him. He said that unfortunately he still heard words such as *gay* and *faggot* on occasion, but not nearly to the extent that he did in middle school, and not directly towards him. Better than that, he found a priest, who was also a psychiatrist, to talk with each week. This gay student said that this priest "really made a difference for me," as this was the first person that he actually formally told that he was gay. He was also able to speak freely with this man and be himself, something that up until now was quite unfamiliar.

Being able to talk with this priest possibly gave this student the boost he needed to tell his mother and stepfather with whom he was living. By the time he was a junior, he had his first homosexual experience and one night when he was feeling particularly "weighed down" emotionally, the secret he had been protecting for so many years slipped out into the open. When his mother and step-father saw that he seemed very upset and down, they asked him what was wrong. He responded with, "I'm gay." It happened that fast. This student went on to describe the immediate awkwardness of the situation as they all sat there looking at each other. This student remembers them responding with, "Well, you're young. You may need more time." This student interpreted their comments as referring to the fact that he was a teenager, and maybe was still confused or unsure about things in general. They thought that it may be a phase. Though this student admittedly "did not know what was going on," knew that it was "definitely not a phase." He chuckled when he remembered thinking to himself, "yeah, I'll need time to meet more guys," and then reflected on the fact that "he had never been attracted to a girl in his entire life."

When thinking back to this moment, this student remembered that his mother and step-father were in no way "surprised," and that they had been aware of all of the teasing in middle school. His mother had even enrolled him in

Karate so he would be better able to defend himself. It was after "coming out" at home, that he decided he should tell his father, whom this student saw every other weekend, and who happened to be an ex-Marine in the United States Armed Forces. He remembers asking his mother to give his ex-Marine Dad a kind of "heads up" before he actually formally told him, though this student didn't predict that his dad would be surprised either. He told his Dad, and his response was something to the effect that, "I will always love you, and you are old enough to make your own *choices*." This student was O.K. with his response, as the nature of their relationship had always been different, and this was as good as he could have hoped for. When he talks about his parents feelings now, he says that, "they are more worried about it than anything. They worry about my life being hard." He continued to say, "and they're right. Being gay is an extra thing that most people don't have to deal with."

When this college student talks about being gay now, he says that "now it's just such a part of me that it's not an issue anymore. It's just one part of the whole person, not everything. I know now that there is so much more to me than that. I have really found who I am and my personality."

As far as challenges or obstacles of being a gay young adult, this student says that one of the toughest things for him has been companionship. He is presently at a small private college, and though he has made many gay friends, he has not found a partner. He says he does not consider himself lonely because he has surrounded himself with people he loves and "who love me back," though sometimes he thinks to himself, "these friends are great, but where is that partner…" Another obstacle, he says, "would be acceptance, not just about other people accepting me for who I am, but for me to accept who I am and that being gay is a part of me." This was one of his biggest challenges through the preteen and high school years, and this student says that, "I am glad that I was through with that process before I got to college."

Before he left to go study, I asked this gay college student what words of wisdom he would have for a teen that may be coming to terms with being gay. First, and foremost, this student would encourage a gay teen to "try not to be afraid, to realize that being gay is only one part of you, and that it is how you are meant to be." He also suggests that a potentially gay teen, "come to grips with his sexuality on his own, and that he should look out for himself as far as entering into an emotionally unsafe situation." The example this student used went back to when he was in the Boy Scouts. He really liked the Boy Scouts and was quite involved for years. He liked the challenges and the new experiences that the Boy Scouts had to offer. Then, one day he remembered reading in the paper that gay men were being banned from being able to be Boy Scout leaders. In fact, it was all over the news. This gay student said that "I would have loved to be a Boy Scout leader, but I would never put myself in that situation, with people thinking that you could be a pedophile just because you're gay."

Lastly, when asked for any advice he would have for parents of a teenager who has just "come out" or who the parents may suspect may be gay, he says that, "you cannot fathom what this kid is going through, and that they need to figure it out first." He continues to say that, "the thought of telling your parents that you are gay is the most petrifying feeling," and that, "parents should be there, but try not to push him." It is also important to realize that if the teen *is* gay, that the process he is going through "really sucks," but that, "it needs to be gone through." By far the most important thing that a parent can do is to, "be supportive, so that he doesn't get discouraged and feel the need to change himself because of what other people think. Cherish him for who he is, so that he will never want to be anyone other than who he is meant to be."

Another college student, a sophomore, told me that things have been so much better for her since she *came out* last year. She said that the first two months of her freshman year were "miserable," that she "hated it," and that she was constantly calling her parents to come and bring her home. Then, this lesbian college student began talking more with her resident assistant, an upper-classmen who manages a certain floor of the dorm, and who also serves as a support and mentor. As she began to speak with her more and more, this student said, "I became more aware of myself and realized what I was really feeling and why I wanted to go home." Once she realized what was really going on inside of her, she says that now she "loves it here." She told her parents this past October, and said, "they took it pretty well. My dad took it the worst at first. He walked out. He was just more upset that something was going to happen to me." When asked how her mother responded, this lesbian young adult said, "she kept asking me if I was *sure*."

When asked about her middle school and high school experiences, this lesbian college student had only good things to say. She attended a catholic school which was K-8 and was with most of the same kids all the way through. She said that she had both male and female friends, but admits to being more comfortable with the guys. She said that she always liked to "play in the dirt," and that she and the guys would talk about sports. She did not date in high school and does not remember being attracted to boys. She chuckled when she told me about all of the posters of Nomar Garciaparra in her bedroom, because looking back she has now realized, "that the posters were all about baseball." This lesbian college student did remember thinking if the fact that she was so athletic could mean that she was a lesbian. I couldn't help but to interject at this point in the interview that this was such a horrible message, in addition to many others of course, that young girls are receiving. It disturbed me to no end that just because a girl is a naturally gifted athlete that she would question her sexuality. She then reflected on her feeling inside saying to herself, "No. That's not it. I'm a lesbian because this is who I am, not because I am a good softball player."

When asked about the challenges of being a lesbian young adult, this student said, "coming out to myself, admitting and accepting that I am a lesbian, then coming out to other people." Now, she says, "that my biggest challenge is going to be telling my parents that I am dating. It will make it real for them. It won't just be a word or a phase." This lesbian college student says that actually things have greatly improved with her parents, and that their relationship is basically the same as it was before she told them, and in some ways she says, "it's closer." She realizes now that her father was "worried out of love."

When I asked her for any advice that she would like to give to a teen or young adult who may be coming to terms with her sexuality she said, "listen to yourself, your heart, the way you are feeling. Don't listen to other people. If it feels right go for it." When asked about what advice she may like to give to the parents of a teen or young adult who has just *come out*, she said, "just listen to them. Ask questions, and always make sure that your kids know that you are there for them no matter what."

So, what do we need to do as parents when our child finds the courage to disclose this very important revelation? According to Haffner, "the most important thing you can do is *listen*. Find out what they are telling you. Ask them to tell you more about their feelings and what they are thinking about their sexual orientation. Some teens may be asking for help in dealing with their confusion about their sexual orientation; others may be telling you something that they have known for a long time. And the other thing you can do right away: Love your child. This is the same teenage child he or she was five minutes before they told you. Tell her you love her. Tell him you will support him. Ask how you can help. Look for a local community center that deals with gay and lesbian youth. Make sure that your gay and lesbian teen can meet adults who are gay and lesbian and who lead successful, fulfilling, and healthy lives."

PART III

Too Much Too Soon-
American Teens on the
Fast Track

*-the power and influence of our media dominated
society*

8

"The Trouble With Normal Is That It Always Gets Worse"

Bruce Cockburn

I facilitate a parent discussion and support group at one of the nearby universities, and one morning we found ourselves straying from the original topic of discussion when a parent asked if they could share a struggle she was having with her teenagers. This mother is a single mom of two daughters, ages fourteen and sixteen, and her frustration was with feeling alone and isolated as far as believing that she had more rules and limits than the parents of her daughters' friends. Then two other parents, with three teenage daughters ages fourteen, sixteen, and nineteen, chimed in that they feel the same frustration. They are constantly hearing their daughters saying, "…well, my friends can all see rated R movies, and my friends are allowed to get dropped off at the Mall", and even worse, " my friends are allowed to be in the car when so and so(teen) is driving. You're so strict!" Many of the parents in the group were nodding their heads in agreement as these parents spoke. They continued to say that they feel *forced* to micro-manage, to say to their teenagers "do this, wear this, watch this…" because things have "gotten so bad."

As far as movies go, most were in agreement that the rating system has changed from three decades ago. The "ante has been upped" one parent commented. Another said that her teen likes to watch the show "Friends" which she feels is very promiscuous. She continued to say that on that show, "everybody sleeps with everybody", and that she didn't want her daughter "taking it all in." Some may think that this is over the top, but there is actually quite a detached sexual epidemic going on in our country right now. Kids nationwide are performing oral sex as young as seventh and eight grade and saying that it is no different than a "kiss goodnight." Even during the 60's when the message was to "make love not war", and young adults dressed in bad clothes were openly expressing themselves sexually, they weren't twelve. For the most part, the oral sex going on is being done by girls to boys, and in places such as the backseats of school buses. Of course movies are not entirely to blame, however, I don't believe it can be disputed that kids are exposed to a great deal more these days than ever before and at much younger ages. In fact, my husband went to rent a movie for our sons (ages ten and thirteen) last Friday night, and he came across "Stand by me", a movie that both of us liked. At the check out counter, he noticed that it was rated "R", and asked the person at the register why. The young man at the register responded with, "Oh, that's an R from the old days. It's not the same as an R today. That movie is fine." The week before that, my husband had rented "Anger Management" for us to watch, rated PG, which had several scenes in it that I would not have wanted my thirteen year old to see or hear, especially the part about "angry masturbating."

We have discussed sex with our oldest two children, and when we did talk about it, it was with meaning and with emphasis on the relationship part. This is the part that is missing for adolescents today. Teens have *always* been run by their hormones, but not to this extreme and not this young. Kids are growing up too fast and too soon, with what appears to be a certain recklessness. Just as they have been desensitized to sex, so it is the same with violence. Most would agree that this is about 99 % due to the screen time that these preteens and teens get each day, not only the T.V. and movies, but the video games as well. Across the nation, teens can be seen staring at these miniature screens with their thumbs frantically waving up and down, oblivious to what is going on around them. Many of these games are as bad, if not worse than what they are watching on television. There is a game out there called "Diablo", a Spanish word for "the devil", where you are actually doing the killing through the eyes of this evil creature, as opposed to two people shooting or stabbing each other (not that this is a good thing either). This is also the game that was found in the basement of the teens' home that were responsible for the Columbine murders.

It used to be that the only places where teachers and parents had to be concerned about guns were in some of the larger inner cities, and these were high schools, not middle schools for the most part, and certainly not elementary schools. This has changed also. Kids as young as six have been caught bringing weapons to school and threatening their classmates and teachers. This has happened so many times, that most schools have modified their behavior codes around it. In most schools, if a student is even subtly verbally threatening there is usually a consequence. Saying something such as, "I really hate Mr. Whoever, and I'd like to get him, " in the old days would probably mean that the teen got a well-deserved bad grade and was afraid to go home and face his parents. He may be fantasizing about setting a paper bag filled with dog poop outside of the teacher's front door then ringing the bell. These days, this could be interpreted as a threat worthy of suspension as there is a lot more reason to worry about what "get him" may mean.

One parent in the group, stated that he thinks that much of the problem lies with parents focusing more on the people in the situation rather than on the dynamics of what is going on. In other words, parents as well as their teens are more focused on the rules than on how allowing ourselves to be in a certain situation can control and dictate our behavior as much as we would like to believe that it wouldn't. His response came following an example that another parent had shared in the group about her teenage daughter being invited to a co-ed sleep-over party. They told their daughter that they did not feel it was appropriate for a sixteen year old girl to be staying overnight with boys, regardless of whether or not the parents were home, and that the answer was *no*. The teenager of course responded with a very predictable, "You don't trust me." These two parents continued to express their frustration to the group saying that they did trust their daughter, and that it was the situation that they did not trust. In fact, they said that she is a very responsible kid who does well in school, however, they simply do not believe their daughter should be staying overnight with the opposite gender at the age of sixteen.

The difficulty was in how to communicate to their teenager that it was not an issue of trust, but one of not being emotionally ready to deal with a potentially tempting situation, as well as the principle of allowing their daughter to participate in something they strongly felt was inappropriate. By not allowing her to go, the message was, "We know that you are unhappy with our decision and probably don't like us very much right now. However, because we love you, we are unwilling to risk you being in an emotionally dangerous situation. It could end up fine, or you could end up in way over your head, and we are not willing to take that chance." These parents said all of this without saying all of this, by their action of not allowing their daughter to go. Not only that, but there is always the possibility with teens that they are nervous themselves, and that they are secretly relieved when deep down inside they know that you are right, though as a parent you will have a better chance of seeing God than them admitting this to you.

We also need to remember that teenagers are going to personalize pretty much everything we say as this is the nature of the teenage beast. They are the axis of their own globes and will remain this way until they are roughly half way through their college years. What we need to do, is to try and redirect the conversation to what the potential consequences may be. We can reinforce the *no* by saying something such as, "We know we can trust you, but what would you do if there was something going on that was making you feel uncomfortable?" Nowhere are we hesitating on our decision, but by inviting the teen to think about potential consequences can be empowering. Even if they opt not to share their thoughts openly at this time, pulling them away from their present moment orientation and directing them to think about consequences within the privacy of their own minds is still a good thing. Kicking this thought process into gear can literally save their life or the life of one of their friends.

Another issue that was brought up by a parent was regarding her daughters' choice of clothing for school. One of the girls came downstairs to breakfast wearing a skimpy, very tight, tank top. Her mother looked up at her and instructed her teenager to go back up the stairs and find something else to wear to school. Followed by the inevitable eye-roll and heavy sigh, she marched upstairs and found something else to wear. This example sparked conversation as every parent in the group seemed to have an opinion about teenage clothes. One parent remarked that it is actually difficult to find anything in stores for girls that covers the tummy area. Much of this is of course due to the teen idols being seen on television and the covers of CD's. Most of the teens will request going to the teenage clothing hot spots, but even some of the department stores that have been around forever have conformed somewhat just to keep in the game. Not only are the middles missing from the young ladies tops, but what is written on them is also different from what was out there thirty years ago. Tops small enough to fit an average nine year old have things written on them saying such things as, "sweet thing, babe, and boy toy." For boys, the phase of wearing pants ten sizes too big so that their boxers underneath can be displayed to all walking behind them, has thankfully left us for the most part. Again, when we are telling our children that a certain outfit is not acceptable to wear, it can help to redirect the focus to what is going on rather than on what they perceive to be a very authoritarian "do what I say." Especially with teenage girls, it can be helpful to explain that we do understand that they want to look attractive, and most of all that they want to fit in. We can say to them, " I completely understand believe it or not. Of course you want to look good and attract the boys, and you are a beautiful and very smart girl, but I just want you to think about who it is you are trying to attract and the kind of attention you'll be getting."

Speaking of attention getting behavior, one thing we may want to address is the fairly recent trend of body piercing and tattooing. Teens and young adults are piercing much more than their ears. This is also a contributing factor to the half shirts being worn by our nation's teenage girls. Many of them want to show off their belly rings, or their belly ring stick-ons when mom and dad will not allow the real thing. Teens everywhere, both boys and girls are piercing their tongues, lower lips, eyebrows, noses, and nipples. More teens and young adults than ever before can be seen walking around with tattoos. The tattoo referred to as the tribal band, is a circular tattoo resembling barbed wire wrapped around the upper arm has become quite popular. Both boys and girls are plucking their eyebrows, and it is more common than not to see a cell phone strapped to the waist of a teen walking ahead of you. In the 50's, the trend was high top sneakers, fast cars, and poodle skirts. In the 60's, it was peace signs, head bands, and long hair. In the 70's, it was a trend of "flashy" big cars, big hair, and big pants. In 2004, the trend is do something self-mutilating, painful, and permanent. The poodle skirts, peace signs, and bell-bottom pants eventually got packed up, thrown away, or sold at yard sales. The tongue, front lip, and nipple rings can thankfully someday be removed. For now, they look painful, not to mention the fact that it is a struggle to understand a teen trying to speak with a pierced tongue. The tattoos, however, will be with our teens when someday they are the grandparents of teens themselves.

After sharing various stories, the group began to question the differences between the teen world of today versus the teen world of the 70's and 80's. Certainly there are many similarities, as developmentally not a lot has changed. The basic theme of the transitional stage between childhood and adulthood where kids struggle to figure out who they are while testing every limit and boundary they have ever known in order to become autonomous and emotionally independent has not changed. What has changed is what teens are faced with in the world today. In fact, another couple in the group talked about their big move to a neighborhood from the outskirts of town. The idea was to have some of what they had growing up when they were pre-teens and teens with a built-in kind of social network, spontaneous neighborhood kick-ball games, and friends just to hang out with after school without having to be planned or driven anywhere. These parents said that, "This has not happened. We have found that the kids are not there. They are either at daycare or after school programs, or scheduled to go to karate or ballet. No one is around until 6:30 in the evening, then of course, we want our own kids in for dinner, homework, and baths. They really don't have any neighborhood friends per say."

Then the group, mainly in their forties, began to talk about things as they were when they were growing up. Most of them grew up in neighborhoods, with the exception of one dad who grew up on a farm. They talked about life being simpler as far as not being so scheduled. "There was far less running around," one parent said. "We could walk to our friends' houses. We played flash light tag in the dark and no one worried that something could happen." Another parent said that, "Our lives revolved around our bicycles, at least in the pre-teen and early teen years. You could tell where everybody was by the bikes lying on the front lawn." Most of the parents agreed that formal activities just did not exist, at least not to the extent that they are available today. Another parent said, "Our parents never drove us anywhere. We had a public pool in town where we hung out all day everyday during the summer. During the rest of the year we had who ever lived within walking distance to be friends with. Parents didn't worry as much. They knew that we were at one of three or four houses. My mother used to yell out the door when it was time for dinner. Wherever I was in the neighborhood I could hear her." Much of this change in kids being physically present, is due to the fact that there are many more two income families. Both parents are working and do not want their preteens and teens to be home alone, so they find sports or activities for them to be involved in. If they are "latch-key" kids, they are usually given a specific set of instructions, which would include staying in the house and doing their homework. There are far more single parent families than there were thirty years ago as well as divorced families sharing custody. Shared custody situations are also part of the reason that many kids are not available on the weekends. These kids often miss birthday parties and other social events because they are *scheduled* to be with their other parent on the weekend, the time kids would usually have to just hang out. Instead, many of them are whisked off to be *entertained* (taken to the movies, mini-golf, to the beach or whatever) when it is the other parent's "turn."

The idea of needing to be entertained is worth discussing for a moment, as this is also something that has changed drastically from three decades a go. Kids who grew up in the 70's and 80's did not have video games, or videos for that matter as the first VCR's didn't come out until the early 80's, at least not for the main stream middle-class. We will even set aside for the moment, the fact that the "ante has been upped", and that the exposure to sex and violence is far worse than it was. We will also set aside the fact that the family system is mocked and the parental role models are frequently disrespected as a form of humor. We can also set aside the language which did not exist at all in shows such as "I Love Lucy", because they relied on sheer talent and did not need it. What we will take a minute to look at, is what the *amount* of screen time is doing to our preteens and teens. The hours of television watched by our youth have been somewhat of a problem for a while now. We are the most overweight nation in the world, with the most overweight children in the world, as there is an obvious strong correlation between a sedentary lifestyle and eating habits.

Now, with so many more two income families, there are many more preteens and teens being left home alone to sit on the couch and zone out to as much T.V. as they want to, or to play video games without limitation. With the invention of the hand held video game, these kids can keep their thumbs frantically flying while they are in the car or waiting at the dentist. This is time that could have been spent picking up a book, drawing, having a conversation, or staring out the car window day dreaming about the future. In my opinion, this is largely contributing to the "detached" nature of our society. It seems that parents are far more out of touch and emotionally disconnected from their children than they used to be, and children are disconnected from each other and their actions. One example of this is that many preteens and teens are treating oral sex as a "kiss goodnight." They are emotionally disconnected from their actions. The fact is that oral sex is still sex. It counts. In addition, there is also the risk taking element that is enhanced by the time spent playing these games. The whole focus of the video game, is to win at a certain level so that you may advance to the next one. The entire focus is "upping the ante."

Of course the video game is not solely responsible for the moral decline in our society, however, it is most definitely a contributing factor, as is the number of hours of television being watched by our children. Children are like sponges in that they soak up everything in their atmosphere, good or bad, and what they are taking in from their television screens is being internalized and affecting their thinking, how they want to look, and their actions. As growth and development are a continuous process, what is going on with our preteens and teens now will very much affect what kind of adult people they will become, which will therefore eventually shape our society and our world. This may be something worth pondering.

9

"Friends With Benefits"

"The new tribes are informal, dynamic, and frequently temporary alliances, centered around 'their members' shared lifestyles and tastes' around feelings rather than a commitment to particular ideologies or beliefs."

—Body Dressing
edited by Joanne Entwistle and Elizabeth Wilson

One result, or might we say casualty of our media-dominated, sex-indulged, society where the majority of our children are being exposed to too much too soon, is what has been termed the *friends with benefits* relationship. I had the very fortunate experience of meeting with one of the leading experts on the subject, Dr. David Landers, Director of the Student Resource Center and Professor of Gender Studies at St. Michael's College in Colchester, Vermont. Dr. Landers who has worked with teenagers and young adults as a college counselor for over 22 years, defines a *friends with benefits* relationship as one in which "people who care about each other and are friends, in some cases becoming sexually active with each other, but who are not looking for a long term relationship." According to Dr. Landers, the *friends with benefits* relationship "may have gotten its start within the gay community because gay people did not have as many options for relationships as the heterosexual community did." He went on to explain that a couple of years ago we began to see more and more of this detached type of relationship among heterosexual people, first amongst our nation's college population, then in our high schools, and now in middle schools as well, something Dr. Landers refers to as the "trickle down affect."

What happens, according to Dr. Landers, is that two people who care about each other as friends "are looking for companionship, and comfort, and in the process of comforting someone else, one or the other person gets sexually aroused. In that process they do something about it." He goes on to explain that the relationship undergoes a change and leaves one or both parties questioning what just happened, as they are "not dating" and were merely "looking for comfort." They find themselves in a situation where their friendship now has some kind of "sexual component." Dr. Landers states that the sexual component can "be as simple as cuddling and kissing, to oral sex, to intercourse, but they are *not* defining themselves as being in a relationship."

The oral sex component is worth focusing on for a moment as the frequency with which it is happening amongst teenagers as well as preteens, is rapidly reaching epidemic proportions. According to Sara Wilson of *The Globe and Mail*, a Canadian-based news source, "School counselors, researchers and teenagers say that girls as young as 12 and 13 are performing oral sex-not just the class 'bad girls,' but girls from every walk of life. They don't consider it real sex, but an act almost as normal as acne and cafeteria gossip." She goes on to say that, "*Fooling around* and *hookups*-terms kids use to describe everything from kissing to groping, mutual masturbation to oral sex-happen when couples are alone, and when they are in peer groups. They happen in stairwells, in bathrooms between third and fourth period, and in the playground at recess. They happen in parks, on class trips and in cabins at camp. They happen at home and at after-school or weekend parties, whether or not parents are out." She explains that these kids are coming from housing projects as well as the suburbs, from schools public and private, and that "in some circles, the act is even de rigueur, an admission ticket to the cool cliques of star athletes or honor students."

Of course, in 1999, almost immediately following President Clinton's public affirmation of oral sex being distinctly different from *actual* sex, and defined oral sex as *sexual relations*, we began to see a mirroring of this attitude in middle school and high school students all over the country as well as a significant increase in our teens and preteens taking part in this act that they are not developmentally nor emotionally ready for. According to Jennifer Warner, of WebMD Medical News Archive, who writes in her article *'Hookups' and Dating Similar to Teens*, that "Whether it's a 'hookup' that happens in the closet at a party with an acquaintance, or a romantic date with a girlfriend or boyfriend, there is a one in four chance that sex will be on the agenda for teenagers. A new survey (released by Kaiser Family Foundation and conducted in 2002 by International Communications Research) shows that about a quarter of teens say that sexual intercourse or oral sex are likely to occur in either situation." Warner continues to say that, "Researchers say the survey shows there is little difference when it comes to what teens are doing sexually in their relationships with the opposite sex, whether it is a casual encounter or part of a long-term relationship. About a quarter of teens said that oral sex and sexual intercourse are a routine part of both types of relationships."

In addition, the oral sex going on is primarily a one way street. Young girls are servicing boys, with the boys rarely returning the favor. Dr. Landers states that, "It is all about the strong need for a sense of belonging." He continues to say that it also comes down to "perception versus reality," in that "if the perception is that everyone is having sex, and you want to fit in, then you are going to have sex." And, he says, that as parents or other influential adults in our children's lives that "we dramatically underestimate the power of peers."

Much of what Dr. Landers sees within the college population, he says started in middle school with girls being sexualized before they were ready and with boys receiving distorted views of masculinity and what it means to be male, a large part due to the influence of mass media. In addition to being confused and influenced by their peers, teenagers are confused by society and often inadvertently by the adults in their lives. Jennifer Johnson, MD., M.S., of Healthology Press, ABC News, says that, "Sexuality is a very important part of who we are, and adolescents who have gone through puberty have the same hormones and the same hormonal drive as adults. And our society reinforces those drives. We do all kinds of direct and indirect things to encourage sexual intercourse and sexual behavior-everything except talk about sexuality. So we're giving our kids a double message." She continues to say that, "On the one hand, we're exposing them to people who have sex, for example on TV, but on TV they don't talk about contraception and don't use condoms." In other words, we are quick to say what *not* to do, but we don't seem to have a lot to say as far as how a teenager "might express their sexuality in a healthy way."

Dr. Landers states that the peer pressure goes from Junior High all the way up, beginning when kids leave elementary school and are told, "You need to grow up." He continues to say that, "We need to look at how we almost force our girls to become sexualized the second they get out of elementary school." Part of this issue has to do with the clothes they are wearing, specifically, the half-shirt. The parents are saying, and rightly so, that they do not want their daughters wearing these shirts. The girls' response has generally been, "look what is available in the stores, and if I don't dress this way than I will be totally different, and I *can't* be different." Dr. Landers says that, "they may dress in a way that they are not comfortable with," and that, "these kids want so badly to fit in that they may act in a sexual way before they are supposed to," and lastly, "that we buy into it." He goes on to say that if parents refuse to allow their kids to wear these clothes, that they will find a way to conceal them and carry them to school, changing in the girls' room when they get there. Dr. Landers mentions that the flirtatious messages inscribed on the front of many of these half-shirts sexualize these girls without them necessarily being consciously aware of the connection between the clothes and the type of attention they are attracting and receiving. Even if they are consciously aware of the sexual attention, they are most likely not ready or able to handle it. Not only are girls wearing shirts with sexually suggestive phrases, but Dr. Landers informs us "that they have recently come out with a line of clothing that is actually *boy-bashing*, saying things such as *boys are evil*," and that he, "finds it quite disturbing."

Dr. Landers explains, that what we find at the college level is a population that has "been sexualized before they were supposed to be," and "with strong misconceptions of what it means to be male or female." Terri Apter, author of *The Myth of Maturity*, also speaks of the mixed messages and confusion in regards to the sexuality of young adults whom she labels *thresholders*. Apter speaks about young adult stories being, "tales of regret and disappointment as often as they are tales of pleasure," and that, "their environments are awash with contradictory messages about sex." She continues to say that, "within the past thirty years, sex has become an expected part of young people's lives. A college that set down dorm rules governing visits by members of the opposite sex would now seem out-of-date and out of touch. At the same time, however, sex is portrayed as fraught with danger. Rape, AIDS, and pregnancy advisory centers are advertised in every library and restroom, where machines dispensing multi-colored condoms are constantly filled", and that, "sexual messages are wrapped with both sophistication and caution. Sex is accepted as no big thing, yet thresholders need constant warnings that it exposes them to attack and disease."

Who wouldn't be confused? Young girl's clothing is sexualizing them as early as nine years old. Billboards, magazines, and sitcoms are loaded with sexual content and giving young girls a very mixed message of "Be strong and go for it. There is power in sexuality. Everybody's doing it. It's no big deal and you don't need to be emotionally committed." At the same time girls are hearing, "Sex is dangerous and risky. You could get pregnant or die of disease." It is your basic *come here-go away* message. It is getting worse and this, for the most part, we can blame on the media. In fact, just recently I was browsing through a music store and could not help but notice one of Brittany Spear's older CD's. She was dressed in an all white, very low cut dress with a cross around her neck, and with a set of very provocative eyes peering out from beneath her loose blonde locks. As an adult I found this confusing, so I can only imagine what may be going on within the subconscious mind of a teenage girl. The picture looked as if she was trying to portray innocence at the same time as wanting to be viewed as a *hot babe,* inviting sexual attention yet at the same time rebuking it. Go figure.

As far as young men, Apter explains that they "are expected to have strong sexual desires, yet are condemned for them. Their social culture is more informal than ever, yet their behavior is policed by accusations of harassment and assault. Young men and women expect to be equal, yet often feel hostile and wary toward one and other. Thresholders' first adult experiences of desire and need occur in a climate that is both political and personal and highly confused on each front. It is not surprising, then, that their sexual feelings are charged with ambivalence."

Add to the confusion and mixed messages of young adult sexuality the on going *perception* of what their peers are doing, and things begin to escalate even further. Their perception of what is going on out there can be real or imagined, as the affect is the same. The social need to belong continues to be a strong force guiding the behavior of these young adults. Dr. Landers says that, "even at this age, the pressure to fit in is incredible." He says that without J. Crew, Abercrombie and Fitch, and L.L. Bean, that "our students would be naked." After a semester goes by, many of them realize that it doesn't matter, but when they first walk in the door, he says, "they just want to fit in." He says that when they arrive on campus for the first day of classes, that both young men and women not only think that they have to dress a certain way, but that they are supposed to behave in a certain way also. Guys walk in with a certain preconception of what their college experience will be, similar to what was portrayed in the movie *Animal House* as well as some of the others that have come out over the past couple of years, with lots of keg parties, and according to Dr. Landers, "thinking that they are going to have sex every night of the week." These college students are "thinking that this is what they are *supposed* to do, even if they don't want to."

For many males entering college, the message is not merely that they are *hoping* to have sex, but that they are *expected* to have sex. This message has become so powerful among these young men, that Dr. Landers began facilitating a workshop during freshman orientation on the subject of sexual assault. He begins by conveying the definition of sexual assault, according to the state of Vermont, via microphone to the incoming freshman class made up of approximately 500 young men and women. He begins by addressing the guys, "Let me give a message to the men in this room. First of all this is the definition of sexual assault in the state of Vermont. Penetration without a person's permission, or if the person is too drunk or stoned to give permission, and that penetration can be with a penis, a finger, a tongue, or another object. Men have to understand that *no* means *no*. It doesn't mean try later. It doesn't mean try harder, and just because you do not hear *no*, that does not mean *yes*. It cannot be any clearer than this."

Now to the young women, Dr. Landers says, "You have got to say what it is that you *do* want to do and what it is that you *do not* want to do. You can not just *assume* that this is what he wants. You may want someone to *hold you and to cuddle with,* and he is looking to *have sex,* because that is how you are constructed and that is how he is constructed. If you do not start saying that I want to do A, B, and C, but I am not doing D, E, F or G, and if you are not clear about what you are willing to do, he is going to take it the wrong way. He will take it the wrong way not because he is a bad person, but because he has gotten the message that this is what he is supposed to be doing, and he also hears a message that this is what you really want. He may be thinking that you are *saying* no, but that you do not really *mean* no, again, not because he is a bad person, but because this is the way that he is wired." Dr. Landers encourages these young women to be as clear as they can be, and even went so far as to suggest that they say something to their partner such as "you have a nice body and I just want to play with it. I don't want to have intercourse with you, and if you try it, I will scream loudly, then charge you with sexual assault, and you will go to jail." Dr. Landers reiterates that this is the level of clarity that young men need.

He further elaborates that it is when clarity is absent, and non-verbal signals are misinterpreted, that we end up with a 'he said-she said situation'. These situations often result in emotional devastation as well as legal consequences. He goes on to say that, "here at the college we have a negotiation process where we present and discuss options as far as dealing with what happened. The general community however, may not be as able to handle a 'he said-she said' situation as well." We are so used to telling men what *not* to do, when what we need to be doing simultaneously, is telling young women to be clear about what it is they *do* want to do. Dr. Landers suggests that parents start discussing sexuality and relationships with their preteens and that they drive home the fact that *no* means *no*. He states that we need to say to our male teens that, "You may not touch her breast. You cannot reach inside of her pants. You cannot *assume* what she wants to do." What we need to say to our female teens is, "Guys are going to try and convince you to do things that you may not want to do, not because they are bad people, but because of how they are wired. Guys and girls think differently." He says, "We also need to drive home the fact that oral sex is indeed sex. Listen to the word o-r-a-l s-e-x. S-e-x is part of the word. Oral sex is sex."

"My concern," explains Dr. Landers, "is that since we are seeing so much more of this behavior at the college level, that it won't be long before there is more of it going on in high schools, and then eventually in middle schools." And, he says, "that in a high school situation, most girls would not have the self-esteem to come forward and say anything, and that it is going to take a very strong young woman to be able to do so." Dr. Landers explains that how the 'he said-she said' situation is related to the *friends with benefits relationship*, in that "there are very few boundaries in this type of relationship. The two people involved are friends, but have not self-defined as going out, and again, she is looking for comfort and he is looking for sex." He continues to say that, "guys get an erection and they think they have to do something with it. They don't always understand that just because they have an erection that it does not mean that they need to find someplace to put it. Then, we throw in the element of alcohol, and all bets are off."

Dr. Landers reiterates that the primary dynamic behind this behavior is, "that people want to belong. Everybody wants to belong, and everybody wants attention. It is human nature and even more so at this stage of development, especially when adolescents and young adults are making the transition from one developmental stage to the next. They are apt to fight authority, to rebel, and to assert their independence." These feelings are developmentally appropriate for this life stage; however, it is how these adolescents and young adults choose to act out these feelings that matters. Many male teens and young men have accumulated verbal messages as well as numerous visual messages from the media that what it means to be male is to be physically strong, dominating, and sexual. In fact, there have been some very high profile 'he said-she said' cases, many involving athletes, where the phrase "boys will be boys" was used. Dr. Landers says that not only is this "no excuse, but that it is an insult to every man." As far as messages to girls and young women, things have certainly changed if we want to compare to the perceptions and attitudes of the 1950's, as far as playing a submissive role in the shadow of men, but we still have a long way to go. Girls and young women are still sexualized, and are still viewed in many instances where the scene mixes sex and violence, and as women in the thousands of battered women's shelters nationwide will say, "I deserved it." Yes, we have made some progress as far as women having a voice, but not enough, and the education and support needs to continue.

When questioned about where this *friends with benefits* trend is going, Dr. Landers answered with, "I think people are going to get really hurt. Men are going to have the expectation that they can do this with everybody. Women are going to think that they are expected to do this with everybody. People are just simply going to get hurt." Dr. Landers states that prevention is the best solution, and that education and communication are the best, and most affective tools as far as conveying the concept of what *friends with benefits* means. He states that, "Education begins at home with parents sitting their preteens down to discuss not simply the various ways of expressing sexuality, but the responsibility of a sexual relationship, and not just physically as far as pregnancy prevention, AIDS, and STD's, but emotional responsibility also."

In addition, Dr. Landers says that parents need to communicate with each other and establish consistent guidelines for what they are willing to allow their preteens and teens to do, where they will be allowed to go, and the rules as far as curfews, who they are allowed or not allowed to be in a car with, and when to call parents to confirm a safe arrival at a social destination. He strongly suggests that parents "get on the same page" as far as establishing the ground rules for house parties, as far as making it clear that no alcohol will be served and that parents will be present, not upstairs reading a book or watching a movie, but actually physically present. Lastly, Dr. Landers suggests that parents not *assume* anything and to keep communication lines open.

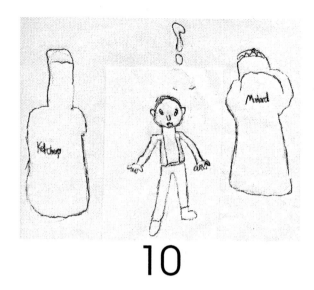

10

Catsup or Mustard?

Why limiting our children's choices is a good thing...

This particular subject is one of passion for me. In fact, I do not believe that it will be terrorism that will bring our country down, but permissive parenting, as we are producing a generation of self-centered, joyless kids, whose appetites for being entertained and stimulated are insatiable. Plain and simply, they are being given *too many* choices and *too much* control before they are developmentally able to handle it, and *not enough* of our time and attention.

Nearly every parenting book out there talks about setting limits and being consistent as this is what children truly need to thrive and feel safe and secure. Our nation has never been richer or fatter and we are throwing cash at our children faster than they can say their first names. In fact, there are now programs being implemented in our public school systems to help prevent childhood obesity as the number of pudgy kids has reached epidemic proportions.

Just a few weeks ago we took our kids to a movie on a rainy Saturday. As I sat there, one overweight child after the other walked down the isle double-fisted with popcorn and candy. I am not normally a weight conscious person nor a detail-oriented person and things need to basically jump out in front of me in order to catch my attention. On this particular day though, I could not help but to notice these overweight kids as they far outnumbered their healthy peers. As far as adults go, the rest of the world has viewed America as the land of the indulgent for years, but the fact that we have now passed this down to our kids has put a different spin on things.

Obviously obesity affects body image and self-esteem for both boys and girls, not to mention the "domino effect" that it will cause them socially with their peers as well as in their new dating worlds. These children are just beginning to figure out who they are and where their place in this world is and they are doing this largely by how others react to them. They are beginning to figure out and explore their sexual selves, and as we all know, adolescence can be and usually is a challenging stage of life with the confusion and emotional highs and lows that it brings. The point here is that we are not doing our children any favors by teaching them to be sedentary and passive. When we let them watch hour after hour of television on beautiful sunny days or when we let them sit on the couch with their thumbs frantically pushing buttons on small electronic devices, we are not being loving, caring, parents.

Even though we may not be harming our children consciously, this is what we are doing. The message to our children is that we do not care enough to make an effort, possibly because we worked all day and it doesn't seem worth it to us to engage in a power struggle with a teenager. Or we may have a very unhealthy need for our child's approval and are avoiding him being upset with us. Either way, the message is the same. Not only are we modeling apathy, but we are also not actively engaging with our preteen or teen. When we allow them to zone out to a screen, whether it is the television, the computer, or a hand held game, we are teaching them that people are not as important as whatever it is they are doing. We are teaching them to be sedentary, passive thinkers, and we are allowing their threshold for excitement and stimulation to increase, creating a child who will get bored very easily when things are not *fun*. This of course impairs the child's ability to grow and mature as part of a being a healthy adult is the ability to delay gratification as well as the ability to commit and follow through with activities or tasks that *need* to be done, though they may not necessarily be *fun*.

There has been a very definite shift in control with this generation. Not only is it unhealthy and a threat to their growth and development, but the self-centeredness that indulgence and permissiveness create, is impairing our children's ability to feel genuine happiness. We are creating a generation of entitled, lazy, unhappy kids by giving them too much materially and too many choices. They do not need or *want*, actually, all of the control we are giving them and we are doing it at younger and younger ages. In fact, I always get a kick out of parents who go on and on explaining to a two or three year old why they should not have hit little so and so, and why her feelings are hurt and yadda, yadda, yadda, when what the toddler really needs is a very firm verbal "knock it off" followed by being scooped up and removed from the playground. These are also usually the parents who offer an entire menu worth of choices to a toddler. They will say to their three year old, "Now Honey, would you like the avocado dip mixed in with your Brazilian vegetarian wrap, or would you like it on the side so that you can mix your brown rice and refried beans in with it, *or* are you feeling more like a chicken burrito with sour cream and a cup of gazpacho?"

Of course, for the most part, these parents are mainly putting on a performance for the people standing in line or at the playground so that they can show that they are educated parents well equipped with the newest innovative ways to raise children. Developmentally, however, they are completely wrong giving a child a lengthy litany of why he or she should not have grabbed a shovel from little so and so or the nine hour offering of lunch options, because the child is developmentally incapable of processing this information. Do they hear their parent? Yes. Do they understand the words? Maybe. What they need, however, are fewer words and a firmer voice so they get that what they did is unacceptable, and not this lengthy discussion in the nicey, nicey voice. The nicey, nicey voice confuses the child. It says, "I am telling you that what you did is unacceptable so please do it again." This is because the nicey, nicey voice is reinforcing to the child. They also need a direct and immediate consequence. Delayed consequences are ineffective as children this age are *right here, right now* oriented. Removal from the scene without toys, snacks, or other children usually works the best.

The reason for bringing up permissiveness with toddlers in a book about teenagers, is because this is where it all starts. The extent of choices that a three-year-old needs begins and ends with whether they would prefer ketchup or mustard on their hot dog. That's it. Of course as kids approach thirteen they should be given a few more choices, but not many more. They are striving to be independent in an effort to make the transition from child to adult, but not nearly as fast or with as much freedom as many of us are allowing them. The result of giving our teens too much too soon is anxiety, lots and lots of anxiety, which in some may manifest as depression. We need to let the leash go gradually, and on occasion we may need to pull it back in again. Our teen's security lies with knowing that their parents are on top of their every move and that we will intervene if we need to. They need to know, that though we may be watching from a distance, that we are indeed watching. Their choices need to have very solid, definite parameters if our teens are going to feel safe and secure. In fact, I have had parents share stories with me about how their teens were actually relieved when they said no to a co-ed sleep over, as they were secretly feeling very uncomfortable but it was too much pressure for them to say so. This way, your teen can say to her friends, "I know. Can you believe what drags my parents are? And I like so wanted to go…," when all the time she is relieved that her parents got her off the hook.

In addition to giving our kids too many choices, another way of indulging them is to *do* too much for them. There are unfortunately many parents out there who are way too focused on their child grabbing a spot in Harvard's freshman class or some other Ivy League school. For many, their child is three or four years old and they are planning a party for the class of 2019. I am thinking that it may be a tad early to send the invitations out, yet they are very much on top of securing that place in the right preschool, some being put on a waiting list over a year in advance. Things have gotten very competitive in our country, as far as the middle and upper-middle classes striving to secure a place for their children in our nation's most elite private schools, with the hope that he or she will be ready to *compete* for that perfect job or that place in medical or law school after they graduate.

Of course we all love our children and want what is best for them, as well as for them to succeed and prosper as adults. I think maybe, that what has changed is how we define success. We have become compulsive about scheduling and *over*-scheduling our children in order to keep up with everybody else, as well as to have everything in place for that prep school application form. Children as young as three and four years old are enrolled in ballet and Tae Kwon Do even though they will have absolutely no memory of the experience by the time they reach adulthood. We are spending a fortune to make our kids neurotic and teaching them that they need to *spend* and *do* to be happy, and as we drive them from one end of town to the other, we are also modeling for them that being drained and exhausted is a desirable state of being. These, in my opinion, are not good messages. Not only that, but we are creating a future generation of runners, children who will grow up completely disconnected from who they are. We are modeling for them that they must be busy every second or something is wrong with them. Something is wrong if they take time for themselves just to be still. In this millennium era, to do *nothing* has become a lost art form, and is affecting us not only as individuals, but as a society and a nation, as we run away from ourselves and each other. It seems that this dynamic is picking up momentum just as a snowball gets bigger and faster as it rolls down hill, and has put the American family on top of the endangered species list.

Our newly acquired need to compete has contributed to our need to indulge our children as far as causing us to be more involved than we should be with things such as homework and soccer practice. There are parents who spend hours going over their preteen's or teen's homework looking for and correcting his or her mistakes, or coming up with ideas for papers and essays. Certainly, I am not saying that we should not help if our teen *asks* for it, but even then we should make absolutely sure that he or she has done all that they can to help themselves. Wayne Rice, author of "Cleared for Take Off" says that, "low self-esteem doesn't come from failing or suffering the consequences of failing. On the contrary, failure has the potential to actually enhance a student's self-esteem if 1) they are given responsibility for overcoming that failure and 2) nobody else interferes in the process. We do kids no favors by rescuing them from their failures and mistakes. They learn best by trial and error, with the emphasis on *error*. If you prevent the error, you prevent the learning. It's really that simple."

We are feeling the need to micro-manage areas of our children's lives where we have no business being, and by doing so are preventing them from learning to do things on their own, the primary requirement for the development of a positive sense of self. We are catching their fish for them instead of teaching them to fish, thereby sabotaging their very natural transition into adulthood.

As far as sports go, it used to be that parents went to *games* to watch their kids, but as far as regular practices go kids were merely dropped of and picked up. It has now become an all too common event for parents to hang around the sidelines watching and offering their tips just for a routine practice. Of course, far worse, is the behavior that has made national headlines where over-involved parents got carried away and brought emotion and violence onto their child's hockey rink scarring all who saw it for a very long time. The emphasis and importance placed on winning is obviously unhealthy, but the mere fact that we are over-involving ourselves and micro-managing so much on the practice level isn't good either. Our teens need and want our time and attention, but not in this way, which is one of the many ways that things get challenging as far as parenting our teenagers. They need us to be engaging and caring about what is going on in their world. What they do not need is to have us in their space leaving them no room to grow. One of our biggest challenges as parents of teens is to find this delicate balance, as well as to have the humility and courage to get back on the horse and try again when we realize that we have messed up.

Dan Kindlon, Ph.D., writes in *Too Much of a Good Thing-Raising Children of Character in an Indulgent Age* that, "Well-meaning parents can end up hurting their children by giving them too much. Too much money, too many toys, too much leeway in how they can behave, too much help, and, too often, unrealistic expectations for about how they will perform in school or on the soccer field." By giving too much in the wrong ways, we are teaching our children that the sun and its planets revolve around them. We are creating a generation of very entitled children, soon to be young adults, who will bring their "what can you do for me attitude" with them to college, then into the job market, and then into their relationships. Many of them will go on to have their own children and the cycle continues, as the majority of this generation, labeled millennials, are not *other-oriented*, creating a generation of parents with even fewer parenting skills than their own parents had.

Not only does indulgence result in entitlement, but it also significantly lowers a child's tolerance to stress and frustration. If we stop to think about this for a minute, it makes perfect sense, as in order to develop the coping skills needed to be able to manage life's difficult and challenging moments, a child needs to be *allowed* to gradually be exposed to some tricky circumstances so that he or she can learn to navigate their own way through or to manage a difficult personality. Kindlon states that, "Indulged children are often less able to cope with stress because their parents have created an atmosphere where their whims are indulged, where they have always assumed…that they're entitled and that life should be a bed of roses." As far as the indulged child's ability to handle frustration, Kindlon continues to say that, "One of the crucial ways in which our sense of self-efficacy can be undermined is when we don't have the ability to handle frustration. Indeed, one of the hallmarks of what we call emotional maturity is the ability not to be fazed by setbacks; to roll with the punches and persevere in the face of difficulties."

I think that is worth taking a look at the connection between this generation of indulged teens and the rapidly rising rates of anxiety and depression. I have spoken with numerous teachers, professors, and school counselors and each one commented on how much things have changed as far as the overall attitudes and behavior of teens and young adults. One college counselor told me that he has never seen so many incoming freshmen on anxiety and depression medication, nor has he ever had so many phone calls from parents to check on them. Many of these same parents called prior to the school year beginning for a list of good therapists in the area so their freshman son or daughter could *continue* their therapy. As I am a therapist myself, I certainly do not want to put a negative spin on a teen seeking out the help and support they need. In fact, I believe it takes an enormous amount of courage to make that first step towards mental health, however, it is the sheer numbers of teens and young adults suffering from anxiety and depression that is the point. Of course, more likely than not, some of these teens are probably struggling with what may be more accurately diagnosed as an *adjustment disorder*. I say this because a child who has been indulged, over-protected, and micro-managed, will most likely struggle with any major change in his or life, such as moving away to college, because they have been prevented from developing any coping skills. It is like telling them to run after being pushed around in a stroller for eighteen years. They would have been much better off had they been allowed to walk first, even falling down a few times and acquiring some bumps and bruises. Why, because this is real life.

As far as teens and young adults who are *truly* anxious and depressed, with the exception of clinical depression or other organically based mental illnesses, the reason for their sadness is many times a lack of parental involvement. Parental neglect happens within each socioeconomic stratum, however, only recently has attention been paid to the more privileged teens and their problems. Many of these teens have double-income, jet setting parents who find it easier to write a check than to be physically present and emotionally available for their children. The message here is obviously that their career is more important than their child which is enough to make any kid depressed. I want to be clear that in no way is this a judgment on career-parents, however, what is often the case, is that parents get caught up in the momentum of their fast paced lives and the kids get left in their wake. Wealthy parents will often throw cash at their kids out of guilt, or apathy, as it is much easier to keep teens happy than to actually take the time to engage with them and find out what is going on in their world, who and what is important to them, what their thoughts on world issues are, their dreams for the future, etc. Of course, in reality, these kids are anything but *happy,* even though they may put up a good front, as they still are teens and teens like cash as it translates directly into freedom. What they are craving is a parent to be interested in who they are becoming and to listen actively to what they have to say. They need to feel that they are worth spending time with. It is when these very basic needs are not met, that a teen gets depressed, and unfortunately with this high risk group, many do not survive it.

In fact, because this new tween and teen generation has been given too much too soon, there has been an actual shift in focus from what used to be an enjoyable, more slow-paced middle-childhood, to kids wishing to get passed it as fast as they can in order to be grown up. These tweens (kids 8 to 14 years old), according to Newsweek's *The Truth About Tweens*, these kids are a "are a generation stuck on fast forward, children in a fearsome hurry to grow up. Instead of playing with Barbies and Legos, they are pondering the vagaries of love on *Dawson's Creek*. The girls wear sexy lingerie and provocative makeup created just for tweens…and boys affect a tough guy swagger-while fretting about when their voices will change." As far as accumulating stuff, *Newsweek* says that, "tweens are a retailer's dream: consumers with a seemingly insatiable desire for the latest in everything…but to parents and teachers, they can also be a nightmare, aping the hair, clothes and makeup of celebrities twice their age while throwing tantrums worthy of a 2-year-old. Psychologists worry that in their rush to *act* like grown-ups, these kids will never really learn to *be* grown-up, confusing the appearance of maturity with the real thing." William Damon, director of the Stanford University on Adolescence says that, "What we're seeing is a superficial sophistication. There's been no increase in the values that help a kid get through the confusion of life in a steady, productive way."

11

Teens, Temptation, and Moral Relativity

"Postmodern societies emerged as a consequence of Modernization, which eventually gave rise to such a high level of existential security that survival came to be taken for granted by growing segments of those societies."

—Ronald Inglehart
Author of Modernization and Postmodernization
—cultural, economic, and political change in 43 societies

Basically, we have become very comfortable as a society. We have it all, per say, and because we no longer have to worry about day to day survival such as we did during the Depression era, we can now focus on our *wants* rather than our *needs*, and those wants have expanded. Relative morality, or *moral relativity*, refers to the shift or change in social norms as far as what we are willing to accept as appropriate feelings and behavior in our world as we know it. Basically, *moral relativity* is the theory that anything goes as long as it does not hurt anyone, which in turn has caused the distance between right and wrong to grow shorter, and the line which differentiates them to become blurry and poorly defined.

I had the opportunity to speak with Dr. Jeff Adams, a professor of psychology at St. Michael's College who has done extensive research in the areas of social personalities and social psychology. Dr. Adams states that this change in social norms, "has a lot to do with the changing role that religion has played in our culture and a need for something to replace religion." Dr. Adams explains that far fewer people these days, when they are struggling with relationship issues or issues of morality, will consult their priest, minister, or rabbi. Most will seek out a therapist, guidance counselor, friend, or the self-help shelf of their local bookstore. For many people, their Church, Synagogue, or alternate place of worship is no longer first anymore, as morality has become very much *secularized*.

Dr. Adams continues to explain, "that because science has in essence replaced religion in many ways, that what we get are called naturalists, or naturalism, one of the perspectives of science, which believes that if we have drives and needs that they are *natural* and therefore part of human nature, which in turn leads us to question why we should suppress them." The result, he continues, "is that we get different perspectives on what is natural. So what happens when we no longer have clearly defined morals and social norms, saying that certain behaviors are *not* acceptable, is people going to the extreme. There are people who are going to take advantage of this because there is money to be made. We have individuals who are looking for ways to make money off of these changes in societal circumstances, looking for something to build or a service to provide that was previously considered immoral but is *no longer* considered immoral. And, even if it is considered *somewhat* immoral, that this item or service cannot be legislated against any longer."

Lawrence Haworth writes in Decadence and Objectivity, that "Growing numbers of people are concerned about our decadence," and that some, "are moved by the realization that although the pace of social change is phenomenal, it is largely without direction. We are careening into the future with little sense of where we are going or what our destination ought to be. In these circumstances, responsible people are mainly managers, caught up in day-to-day problems created by the blind journey. Preoccupied with dodging obstacles immediately ahead and with keeping us more or less upright, they have no time, energy, or capability for bringing overall coherence to the changes that wash over us." Haworth further states that when we consider the social system to be "meaning-less, directionless, and self-destructive-these are reflections that move people to the edge of decadence. By these different routes, they arrive at a common need. To find meaning and direction, and to avoid self-destruction, a compelling image of the future is required, a model of the human world as it might be and as we would like it to be."

Haworth continues to discuss focal value of a society, "as a feature of all of its major purposes, the feature that accounts for their being pursued. Thus, many idealizations of Western society represent it as ordered by the focal value of con-sumption. Consuming is seen as the activity that members of the society regard as finally valuable, and the significance of the characteristic practices is associated with their manner of contributing to or distracting from consumption." If we take an honest look at what makes us *tick* as a society, I think that most of us would agree that we are largely motivated by what brings in the cash, as we con-tinue to be a materialistic society. We like stuff. We like to spend. As far as being stimulated, we like that, too, as most consumer reports would validate the large volumes of sales of movies and video games containing sex and violence. As far as political controversy, we like that also, as was made apparent by the record break-ing sales of Michael Moore's documentary film *Fahrenheit 911*. Our society strives for and enjoys the *extreme*. We look for and reinforce that which *stands out*.

For the most part, we perceive more as better, and certainly this is true of our nation's teens. Their threshold for excitement and stimulation is constantly being raised as the ante continues to be upped. For example, when we look at the movie industry, Dr. Adams says that, "as far as the depiction of relationships, movies would not sell if what we were viewing were warm, every day, companionable individuals living boring, yet comfortable and trusting lives. People won't make movies of those things. Something has to happen because people like to see peo-ple fight with each other. They like to see sex and violence because they find it stimulating. They like to see extremes and adversity, and therefore, this is what sells. Now, what has happened socially, is the norms that depict what is socially acceptable are becoming more and more liberal." Dr. Adams continues, "that somewhere along the line someone decided to teach this inane moral point of view which says that anything is o.k. as long as it does not hurt anybody, which is more or less considered moral relativity or relative morality." What this in turn gives people permission to do, says Dr. Adams, is to say things such as, "then don't go to my movies or listen to my music, but I am still going to make it and you can't stop me." It is all about supply and demand and about *showing us the money*. This generously liberal shift in our social norms, for the most part, has caused social responsibility, as far as creating, advertising, and marketing, to all but vanish, with the responsibility being entirely transferred to the consumer.

This in turn brings up the issue of *choice*, and why people make choices that they *know* are not good for them. Specifically, when we discuss teenagers and their ability to make choices, most psychologists would agree that they do not have the cognitive abilities of an adult. They are very much on their way, and may have moments of cognitive clarity and abstract thinking, however for the most part, they do not yet have the ability to see around the corner. In addition, Dr. Adams says that, "teenagers do not yet have the experience that forces you to consider things. It is not just the experience in terms of what I see and what I do, but the experience in terms of someone actually presenting other perspectives forcing the teen to think things through. It is the *what if* type thinking that they are unable to process."

Dr. Adams goes on to explain a hypothetical example of a fourteen-year-old who asks his parents if he can go on a date, and questions just how deeply a teenager would be able to think about what a date might be like. The reason, Dr. Adams says, "is that they do not have the experience to draw from." He states that, "these teens have the capacity to think deeply in the areas of science and mathematics, but they do not get moral instruction in school. That is the role of the parents." He goes on to discuss that there is also a difference between simply saying this is right or this is wrong, and actually sitting down with the teenager and asking her to talk about why a certain behavior may not be acceptable, what the consequences might be for herself and the others involved, and what her intentions are. Dr. Adams explains that teens by nature are impulsive and need to be guided as far as seeing around the corner, and that the key issue for parents to realize is that they really *believe* they have already thought things through.

Further, it is also important to shift their thinking from internal to the external circumstances that will be governing their behavior. More than likely, if a teenager is questioned about a party, whether or not parents will be chaperoning, which of their friends will be there, etc, they will respond defensively. Of course, the very obvious reason is that teens are the axis of their own globes and will interpret a parent telling them *no* as that parent does not trust them. This is when the parent will need to guide their teen cognitively into thinking about what might happen if the party or social situation becomes overwhelming. The parent can question the teen on what he would do if the whole group decided to leave or do something that he knew was wrong, and what would they do if a situation were to become sexually uncomfortable, or they witnessed someone in an uncomfortable situation. The parent can actually guide their teen into thinking about the *what if* type situations that they would be unable to do by themselves. Teens need a visual, and they need the mental rehearsals with the hypothetical *what if* thinking as they do not have any experience to draw on.

Dr. Adams defines temptation as "being in a situation where a person has both physical and social opportunities which make them aware of certain pleasures, and draw out reactions which they may or may not be able to control." As discussed earlier, tweens and teenagers are often unable to realize that a certain situation may lead to bad circumstances, as their *teen tunnel vision* prohibits them from being able to see around the corner from their actions. What we have at this point, therefore, are circumstances where the concepts of what is right and what is wrong have become loosely defined and malleable, circumstances which are now making the teenager aware of certain urges and desires, without the life experience, ego strength, or coping skills to control these impulses.

In addition, we have the teenager's natural and developmentally appropriate inclination to yearn and struggle for independence and autonomy, where they will begin to actively attempt to pull away from their parents. The teen will now gradually begin to have an increased awareness of physical pleasure and with a very natural desire to satisfy these urges, coupled with the omnipotent pressure to fit in and be liked and approved of by their peer group. They will not only begin to look to their peers for information, validation, and support, but will actually look to their peers to define their new reality. The messages that they will receive from their peers through the mirroring of their own comments and actions will greatly affect how they think and feel about themselves. Dr. Adams explains that, "these kids are moving away. They are looking to be independent from the rules and the rules are established by family. They then move towards their friends, not really understanding that they are becoming more dependent on their friends than they were on their parents."

To what degree these teens allow themselves to be influenced has a whole lot to do with what they have received emotionally from their families throughout their early childhoods. In fact, most psychologists and child development experts would agree that a solid self-esteem remains to be the best prevention against drug and alcohol abuse, smoking, and unplanned pregnancy. Of course, in no way does this mean that a child from a significantly dysfunctional family is destined to continue the cycle of dysfunction, as most of us know adults who have managed to rise above their childhood pain, abuse and abandonment issues to become happy and well adjusted. In fact these *survivors* are often emotionally strong with very empathetic character, however, very few would dispute that these *survivors* are more the exception than the rule. For the most part, kids who lack a strong connection and solid emotional bond with their parents or primary caregivers tend to struggle greatly when they encounter adolescence. Waking up in the morning and going through an entire day being fifteen years old is difficult enough under ideal circumstances, never mind trying to muddle through the uncertainty, confusion, and turbulence without the cumulative security of the parent-child connection, and the foundation of unconditional love and attachment.

Basically, when we speak of the casualties of adolescence, we are primarily speaking of the results of bad choices. We think of a boy coerced into trying his first cigarette, or a girl who did something she was not ready for on a date so that a boy would like her or just to feel grownup. We think of our teens being persuaded to do things that they know are wrong or that are unsafe just to belong, the ultimate nightmare being a teen getting into a car with a friend who has been drinking. Angry teens are often tempted to rebel by challenging authority and rules, as their anger exacerbates their undenied feelings of invincibility. These teens enjoy living on the edge, and often engage in high-risk activities such as drag racing over hills at blurred velocities or accepting the challenge of dangerous dares offered by their peers. We worry about our kids not being able to resist these *temptations*, to resist the forces that cause good kids to make bad choices.

When he speaks of college students, Dr. Adams says that he wonders what has happened to their ability to recognize a situation as one that could lead to bad circumstances. He continues to express his concern and discomfort when he talks about the style of dress of these young women. Dr. Adams explains that is not an issue of self-control but rather an issue of distraction and inappropriateness. He says that there are roughly 25 to 30 students in his class, 85% to 90% of whom are female, as this is the current tendency with courses in psychology. "It is a sea of cleavage," says Dr. Adams, "as this is the style right now for young women, and it is distracting from what I am trying to accomplish." Dr. Adams further discusses the overt sexual expression of the dance teams, which have all but replaced the traditional cheerleading teams for the college's basketball games. Dr. Adam's enjoys attending the games, and says that when the dance team made its debut performance that, "I couldn't believe it. Watching the dance routine was like watching a strip tease. There was a lot of shoulder shaking and a lot of hip thrusting. They were all sexual moves." Also present at this basketball game were Dr. Adams' wife and two children, ages 8 and 11, and Dr. Adams says that, "my wife was covering our son's eyes. What was most upsetting, was that he was seeing these young women *want* to be objectified, and to be related to purely on a sexual level. To be attracted to someone on a physical level is certainly not a bad thing, but when it is in conjunction with the emotional." The message here was that, "I am going to be attractive to you purely on a physical level."

On the parenting end of things, Dr. Adams says that, "parents need to know what it is they want their kids to resist, but they also have to know why, for themselves." Teenagers have graduated from the simple early childhood responses such as "because I said so" or "because it's not safe," which are enough for younger children and tend to work quite well as long as they are delivered with a deliberate tone of voice. Younger children tend to pick up on the strength and confidence of the parent with these firm and concise behavioral directions which in turn makes them feel safe and secure. In fact, too much explanation at this age can impair the child's ability to redirect his or her behavior as it is too much to process. Teens on the other hand, have a newly developed cognitive and emotional need to know what is going on. They need a new level of elaboration in order to feel the same feelings of confidence and security from their parents. What has not changed since early childhood, is that teens still have a strong need to feel that their parents are on top of their game, so to speak. They need to feel that connection, but at a new and different level.

Dr. Adams, from the perspective of social psychology discusses the dynamics of social situations and questions how much of our teens' behavior is governed by their own independent thinking, and how much is governed by the dynamics of the social setting. In essence, he says that social psychology asks, "how much of your behavior is determined by you and who you are, with your values and choices, versus the situation." He explains that, "certain situations can take you outside of yourself, and that your own personality and values, unless you are an individual who has the characteristic of introspection to judge what is going on, and question whether it conflicts with who you are and what your values are, can get drawn in to what is going on. A lot of people are not that way at all, and some situations take *everyone* and pull you right in to what is going on. What happens is people are having fun and get lost in the momentum of the situation." What we need to do as parents, as we *do* have an acquired ability as adults to see around the corner, is to pay attention to these dynamics, and explain to our teen that we are not monitoring *them*, but the *situation*. We need to make sure that our teen is not entering into a situation where the dynamics may become overwhelming, and where he or she will therefore be *tempted* by the momentum of external social forces to be pulled away from their own values and ability to think independently.

12

And by the way, this one doesn't rub off...

✦

-a conversation with a New York Tattoo Artist

"*Fashion, as a material process, involves a good deal more than the symbolic manipulation of codes: as a means of clothing, adorning and otherwise decorating the body, fashion operates at an affectual as well as symbolic level, helping to construct and reconstruct individual subjectivities, whilst simul-*

taneously forging an affectual or experimental relationship between the various actors involved."

—Body Dressing
edited by Joanne Entwistle and Elizabeth Wilson

As strange as it may seem, with all of the heated discussion about body piercing and tattoos, very little of the information, if any, has come straight from the *horse's mouth.* I had the very pleasurable experience of speaking with a *tattoo artist*, as she prefers to be called, from New York and was able to learn of what is going on currently in the tattoo world.

There has certainly been a lot of talk and parental fear about where this trend is going and what got it started in the first place. The most recent trends have been funky hair-doos, colorful hair-doos, big pants, low-riding pants with boxer shorts exposure, half-shirts and hip-hugger jeans, skateboards, and scooters. That is, until a few years ago when the temporary trends became *permanent.* In fact, the very definition of trend means something that becomes popular for a while, capturing the attention and wallets of teen consumers, then very gracefully and appropriately fades into oblivion with the trends of old. The big pants and skateboards land on the same yard sale table that vinyl platform shoes, CB radios, and Eight-track tapes did years ago.

To begin with, New York Tattoo Artist informed me that New York Law prohibits anyone under the age of eighteen to get a tattoo, though there are presently no laws for body piercing. She informs me that in her shop there is a form that must be filled out, signed by a parent, and then be notarized with the raised seal before they will allow a minor to receive a body piercing. New York Tattoo Artist also informed me, that even *with* parental approval, they will turn down a minor if they are too young, or if their body is still too underdeveloped for the piercing they are requesting, most commonly the navel ring. Something else that I was certainly unaware of is that some tattoo shops are members of something called the APT, which stands for the *Alliance of Professional Tattooists.* In order for a tattoo shop to be a member of this organization, they must attend an annual eight-hour seminar followed by a test that each tattooist must pass. If you are a parent who happens to be o.k. with your teen getting a tattoo or piercing, you may want to inquire as to whether the tattoo shop you have chosen is APT certified.

My intentions with interviewing a tattoo artist were simply to *inform* parents, in reporter-like fashion of what is going on out there, so that they know what is walking through the doors of tattoo shops at this very moment. It seems that the age-old cliché of *knowledge is power* would also be applicable here, as to be educated and aware of the current goings on in the teen world can only benefit us as parents. Not surprisingly, many of the tattoos and piercings being done are specific to gender, as well as to certain age groups. According to New York Tattoo Artist, the hot spot for older teen and young adult females is the lower back. Some request tiny ones and some want bigger ones, "not realizing how big they will be," she tells me. As far as the youngest age group, who are allowed to get piercings, the popular piercing of choice is the tongue ring. New York Tattoo Artist says that for both genders, ages 15-25, this is the thing to do. When I asked her why she thought so many teens were requesting to have a needle stuck through their tongues, she responded with, "I think they do it mainly because they know that it irritates the heck out of everybody, however, many of them also do it for sexual pleasure." She continues to describe these teens as they sit there waiting to be pierced as well as educated on what the process involves. New York Tattoo Artist says that, "You can tell that their hearts are pounding away. They are usually clammy. They also know that it's going to hurt and that they may throw up, but they want what they want. That's it."

Young males, primarily in their late teens and early twenties, are getting nipple rings. New York tattoo Artist says that, "they like the way it looks. Young women are getting them, too, but not nearly as many, and not until their late twenties or early thirties. It is primarily the young guys getting these." As far as the older group, meaning people in their 40's and 50's, New York Tattoo Artist says, "we do a lot of cover-ups, old tattoos that they don't like or want anymore. We try to work a new design over the old one. This is also the group that requests most of the private piercings, meaning vaginal and penis piercings. You would be surprised. Most of the clients requesting private piercings are professionals, kind of upscale people. We have had business people, doctors, and lawyers come in to get these. And actually, most of the private piercings we do are vaginal. It seems to be the older, professional women who are looking to enhance their sexual pleasure."

As far as the *permanency* of a tattoo, New York Tattoo Artist had a lot to say, especially after the Twin Towers went down on 9/11. She informed me of the volumes of teens and young adults who came into the shop following the catastrophic terrorist hit on New York City. She told me that most of these "kids" as well as adults were talking about what had happened, and in the same breath were talking of the need for something permanent and secure. Firefighters came in to get tattoos with the numbers 9-1-1 and the image of the towers behind it. New York Tattoo Artist tells me that, "we did lots of flags, especially tattoos with the flag and the Twin Towers combined. We also had firefighters coming in wanting these same tattoos only with names and dates underneath. It seemed like people wanted some kind of memorial, something they could take with them." Separate from the 9/11 event, New York Tattoo Artist told me that she has had people come in who have lost a loved one, and wanted to have something done in memory of that person. Most recently she had a father come in with his brother, whose infant son had just died at only ten days old. He wanted the boy's name tattooed on his upper arm. She also had a dad come in who had lost his adult son. He was carrying a picture of his son with him, and requested the same tattoo that had been on his son's arm to remember him by. New York Tattoo Artist says that, "Although tattoos are certainly not for everyone, that for some, they give a comfort that you really can't get from anything else because they are so permanent."

Of course on the flip side of permanency, where many parental fears lie, is the fact that so much emotional, as well as physical growth happens in late adolescence and young adulthood. Most of us, who are further down the road, will admit that we are not the same people at 24 that we were at 18. This is true all the way through our life-journey, however, from the age of 18 until about the age of 24, there is an actual emotional growth spurt that takes place. Of course this is also why most parents panic when their young adult comes home and announces that they are in love. As parents, we are holding our breath while we silently, or maybe not so silently say, "sure you are honey." We then proceed to go upstairs and say 4,000 consecutive Novenas, or other prayers of choice, in hopes that there will be some kind of Divine Intervention (or sabotage) that will prevent our all-knowing little darlings from making a huge mistake. This is obviously also the reason why we stay up until all hours of the night when our teens are "out." We worry about unprotected sex causing a permanent life change, as well as the potential life changing injuries or death that can result from drinking and driving. *Permanency* makes people nervous, especially if they are not ready for it, and for good reason.

This is why at this particular tattoo shop when teens come in for a tattoo or piercing they are slowed down. New York Tattoo Artist tells me that they have a discussion with the teen or young adult first. The discussion includes information on exactly what is involved in the tattoo or piercing process. She tells me that, "these kids think that it is like getting an earring at the mall. Then they find out otherwise and many of them get angry. My own theory on that one is that kids today just aren't used to hearing the word *no*. They have this attitude that their own parents don't say *no* to them, so who are we to tell them that they cannot have what they want. That's what it is about, too. It's about not being able to get what they want, and they want it yesterday. We do say no, however, if the teen is not an appropriate candidate for a tattoo or piercing. If they are only one month from their eighteenth birthday we tell them to come back in a month. In fact, one thing that we find interesting is when parents get upset with us. We have had parents bring in their fifteen-year-old daughters to get navel rings and then get upset when we tell them that she is still too small, and that her body is still too underdeveloped. Some of the parents can be very entitled." Then New York Tattoo Artist continues, "Though worse than that scenario, is when these mothers come in to get navel rings or tattoos and they have their young children with them. Even though I have my back to the child and they can't actually see what I am doing, it is very awkward and uncomfortable because I can tell that they are upset. They don't understand. I wish that these parents would re-think things before they bring a five-year old into a tattoo shop."

PART IV
Teens Slipping Through The Cracks

-the connection to disconnection

13

Teen Addicts and Alcoholics

We admitted that we were powerless over alcohol, and that our lives had become unmanageable.

—Step One-Twelve Steps of Alcoholics Anonymous

Most *recovering* alcoholics will admit that the only way to remain sober for the long term is to work the program of Alcoholics Anonymous. This is how millions and millions of broken spirits and ruined lives have found their way back, and it is through this program where alcoholics and addicts who are further down the road of recovery help those who have just barely stumbled in the door. At the beginning of each meeting, the speaker will ask if there are any *newcomers*. This person will then say their name followed by their newly acknowledged title of

"…and I am an alcoholic." The group will then greet the newcomer. Shortly thereafter, the new person will acquire a sponsor who will serve as their primary support person should the newcomer feel the desire to *pick up*. The sponsor will also help to educate and guide the newcomer in working the Twelve Steps of Alcoholics Anonymous. Many other recovering alcoholics will often approach the newcomer and offer their phone numbers should he or she need to talk.

As difficult as this can be for adults, the teenager is in the unique situation of not being *finished* yet. They are half-baked bread, still mushy in the middle and in need of a few more minutes to rise. How then, exactly, does a teenager acknowledge *powerlessness* at a time when developmentally, they are struggling to become empowered as they transition to adulthood? These two opposing forces within the teen alcoholic can create additional turbulence where inside their world has already caved in, many times over.

It is difficult enough for a teenager to admit they do not have control over a situation. This is why their very typical response to a parent when they are told that they cannot attend a certain party or other questionable social event, will often respond with, "You don't trust me." This is their way of declaring that they have grown-up, and therefore have full control over their destinies, so we parents needn't worry. Of course, as parents we realize that it is not so much a matter of trust, but more about outside circumstances becoming too overwhelming for even the most confident of teens to handle. As we do have this ability to see around the corner, we come back with either a very simple and direct "No," or some other plan to exert covert control from parental headquarters. For a teen alcoholic or addict, this situation is further complicated, as they are not being asked if they can handle a certain *regular* situation. They are being asked to admit that they are a complete mess, and that they are not in control. Whether the teen is male or female, this is a form of teenage castration, as they are being stripped of any and all sense of power and virility. And if that is not enough, whatever control they did manage to hang on to is about to be taken away.

This is because, part of recovery also involves making changes in your "people, places, and things." If there was certain music that your teen listened to when she drank, then those CD's need to be shipped off to the Salvation Army, or they may need to find their way to the nearest dumpster. If there was a certain group of people that your teen used to drink with, then they no longer can hang out together, even if there is no drinking involved. It is the *association* with drinking that needs to change and be avoided.

I had the very fortunate experience of meeting with Mr. Jim Lawler, an original pioneer of *Student Assistance* and an expert in the field of Addictions Treatment for almost thirty years. He is currently working with kids in an urban school system just outside the New York Metropolitan area. Mr. Lawler works with students Kindergarten through grade twelve and balances his schedule between the elementary, middle, and high schools of this city that is located next to a city which has the highest murder rate per capita in the nation. Because of the close proximity to this city, as well as to New York City itself, there is heavy gang influence in this area and it is infested with drug dealers. Mr. Lawler tells me that there are African-American gangs, Puerto Rican gangs, Mexican gangs, Russian gangs, and every kind of gang that can be thought up. There are "Bloods" and "Cribs." He tells me, "You name it and we've got it." He also explains to me that there is a lot of "MTV and Gangster Rap influence," and that "kids are trying hard to emulate what they are seeing."

As far as drugs and alcohol are concerned, Mr. Lawler tells me that as far as what is going on out there right now, "there is XTC and Coke. Weed is always around. More kids are chipping away at heroin than there were five years ago, but alcohol, alcohol is still number one. It always has been and always will be." Mr. Lawler says, "that when I get a kid who comes to me on heroin, I am honest. I am always honest. I talk about the risk of AIDS and sharing needles. Then I take them for ride down 'crack street' downtown and show them the heroin addicts. It's not so much about fear as it is about reality. Kids doing drugs can't process fear. They need reality. They need to associate negative experiences with their behavior. Then I tell them that they can have it all. They can live on the street, sell their bodies, share needles, and get AIDS, and then worry about dying in six months. They can have it if they want it. Again, it's a reality thing. Then I take them to talk with some recovering addicts so they can see the other side of the disease. I show them that becoming mentally healthy is also *reality*. I give them hope."

Then Mr. Lawler continues, "If you ask me, adolescence is a disease in and of itself. The adolescent brain is not fully developed. The body wants to do its own thing. All we can do is set up guidelines and be consistent. That's the main thing, being consistent. These kids are not used to anyone being consistent with them, which is why, I am sure, that we are seeing such a huge increase in sociopathic behavior. It's behavior without conscience. We are seeing much more aggressive behavior with a whole lot less concern as far as the effects on other people. These kids think that it is o.k. to cheat, whether it's in a relationship or a test. There is an overall lack of morality going on. They just don't care. And trust me, I am no preacher. But we can see it across the boards-across the nation."

Mr. Lawler attributes a lot of this conscience-less behavior to what he has labeled the "computer disease," meaning the large amount of screen time that these kids are getting. Much of the free time of our nation's preteens and teens is being spent playing video games or watching television, and for the most part unsupervised and uncensored. Mr. Lawler said, "I don't think we can even guess what the long term affect will be on these kids from all of the computer time they are getting. Before long, we will need *computer rehabs*. It is the addiction of the future. Many of the kids that walk into my office have no idea how to actually engage with another human being. Not only that, but there is a computer subculture that has developed amongst the kids. They spend their free time during school strategizing over whatever game is the hottest thing, and they sneak around *hacking*, you know, trying to break into people's files. No one reads anymore. I'm telling you. Computers are the addiction of the future, and it's not just the kids. Many adults are getting crazy with it also."

As far as the treatment of these kids is concerned, as a pioneer in the field of Student Assistance, Mr. Lawler has initiated several programs, one of which is *Families Anonymous*. *Families Anonymous* is a 12-Step program just like all of the other *Anonymous* programs. This program, however, is unique in that it is geared towards offering support to parents and significant adults who have a teen in trouble, meaning actively using and abusing drugs or alcohol, actively abusing someone else in the household, stealing, lying, and any other self-destructive behavior. This program serves to help parents get a grip on themselves and their sanity in order that they are in a better place to be able to help their teen in trouble. These chemically dependent teens frequently bring their own internal chaos into their homes. They have a very tightly knit group of peers who are well versed at teaching each other new and improved ways to lie and manipulate their parents in order to do their behavior effectively. Basically, teens using drugs and alcohol are experts at helping each other out. They are also very good at helping each other isolate their parents, further preventing them from intervening and throwing a wrench into the addicted behavior.

Mr. Lawler says that he read about this program going on in California, and that it was working out with a high degree of success, so he brought the idea back to his own school system, and tells me, "It has been going strong for almost twenty years now. It's a good thing because parents get to meet other parents who have been through the system with their kid. The other parents know what it is like to feel isolated and manipulated. They know what it's like to be ripped off. Often times, parents are trying to go with a memory of how their parents did things, and they find that it just isn't enough. They need the support of other parents who know how they feel, other parents who have been there. A lot of it is that they might be learning how to parent for the first time. These kids who are actively drinking and drugging seek total power. They manipulate in any way possible to be able to do their thing."

Mr. Lawler continues, "They come in desperate for some help, after trying the nicey, nicey approach with their teen which of course bottoms out, and these other parents help them to see that it's about limits, and consistency. Parents who have progressed help the new parents together, to see and take a more *tough love* approach. They know the strategies that work to sabotage the teen's attempt to gain control over the family and the household. They also know which rehabs are the best, and which ones are not. They know how to seek out and find good aftercare. They know who are the good therapists and those who are shaky. We also have situations where one parent may come in initially to get stronger, and then ends up bringing their spouse in down the road. We help them to get the help they need on the outside as well. Many of these parents have their own therapy work to do. It's tough to parent if you're emotionally an adolescent yourself. This is a great program. It's about parents helping other parents and it's going strong."

Mr. Lawler also started the very first *Narcotics Anonymous* support group in his district, which has also been going strong for quite some time. As far as getting kids involved in NA, Mr. Lawler tells me that it is challenging as the outside support groups for the most part are "dominated by older people. So what we do is to try to continually get young peoples' groups going. And to be honest with you, we have to keep at it. Kids have a tendency to slip. They are surrounded by it. It's everywhere. Not only that, but they don't even know when they have hit rock bottom. Their feelings are numbed out. They don't have the ability to process this. They may have had a few near car accidents and a friend die directly due to alcohol and they still don't get it. As I stated before, adolescence itself is a disease. These kids are not finished yet, which is why treatment can be challenging. We need to keep the mentality that we are in it for the long term. They might stay sober for a while and do well, then slip, then come back. It's all about the long term. We keep at it and hope that it sticks. What's great is when it does. That's what we're in it for. I am very passionate about what I do, but to do this, you have to be willing to go the distance. The job is not over when the school bell rings."

Mr. Lawler explains to me that, in essence, the whole goal or purpose of the Student Assistance program is to recognize and treat *high-risk* kids. He says that, "We want to get as many kids, and families as possible on the road to mental health. More often than not, there has been multigenerational substance abuse. These kids who come from alcoholic families suddenly discover the elixir of drinking and it is like they develop an allergy to it. They wonder what happened. Of course there has been a lot of discussion as far as the disease model of addiction, and I can tell you that in the twenty-eight years that I have been working in this field, that I have definitely seen some truth to that. That certainly is not all there is to it, but there is definitely a biochemical or genetic trait that is being passed down."

Kids will walk into Mr. Lawler's office "wanting to talk, and wanting someone to listen. Nobody is listening to these kids. They trust me. I have basically raised many of these kids from Kindergarten, then they come to me when they are in middle school or high school wanting to talk about what happened at a party that they went to over the weekend. One kid might have had too much to drink and thrown up, but be really embarrassed talking about it. Another kid might have done the same thing and be thinking and rationalizing about how he'll handle it next weekend. He may just plan on trying to drink less. This is the kid I'd be watching. This is a definite flag. Then I'd bring him in and talk with him about who he is hanging out with, and the behaviors that are resulting from his drinking or drugging. Often the behavior is out of control. We then bring in the parent, or parents, and have an intervention in my office. I will also go out into the home if necessary. The goal is to get people into treatment. When you put the energy out there, there is always spin off from it."

Mr. Lawler continues, "Of course, as I mentioned previously, after bringing the kid's family in, what I find more often than not is that what we have got is a situation where basically older adolescents are parenting younger adolescents. Alcoholism may go back several generations, and of course if the kid's parents were raised in an alcoholic home themselves, there will be very few if any parenting skills there to speak of. If these parents were self-medicating also, then they were unable to get what they needed from the adolescent life stage. They grew older in age, but did not grow on the inside. They did not learn the life lessons of adolescence, primarily socialization, communication skills, and intimacy. These parents have missed out on all of the developmental cues, and for the most part their self-worth is in the toilet. They are nothing more than 'older adolescents', who are masquerading around as adults with basically no communication skills and virtually no ability to be intimate. Not only that, but because they have such a strong fear of intimacy, they are often left with anger and some very rigid boundaries."

When asked how Addictions Treatment has changed over the past few decades, Mr. Lawler responded with, "Well, Managed Care has pretty much screwed it all up. The kids that we do end up sending off to inpatient treatment facilities need long term support. It used to be that they were in there for 60 to 90 days. Then when they got out there was an after-care program with group and individual therapy. They need this support to make it work and stay sober. Now, we are lucky to get a kid into a rehab for more than ten days. That is the standard amount of time, ten days, and there is no more aftercare just ready and waiting. It used to be that insurance took care off all of this, and now they can't get these kids out of there fast enough. And the thing is, kids do have a tendency to slip. It's the life stage. They are surrounded by it and the pressure of their peers can be too much. It can be challenging." When I asked Mr. Lawler what a parent should do if they suspect that their teen is using drugs or alcohol, he responded with, "get yourself the help you need first, then go from there."

14

The Cyber-Teen

✦

-teens using the Internet as a means of bullying, escapism, anti-social socializing, safe dating, sexual exploration and addiction

Little moral development transpires through machines-moral development is a human occupation.

—Michael Gurian
Author of *The Good Son*

The Internet has opened up a whole new dimension for us. We now have basically unlimited access to information and people the world over with very limited checks and balances. It seems that since the Web is still somewhat in its infancy stage, the part where people are forced to be accountable for their actions by external rules and legislation has not yet caught up. It is only recently that Internet Law has become a career choice for eager young attorneys. Anyone out there with too much time on their hands can write cruel and scathing reviews on anyone else's professional web-site. Some of the most common victims of cyber-terrorism are small business people, artists, authors, workshop facilitators, and anyone else who provides a service for a business. Basically, anyone who has created a professional web-site is vulnerable. This abuse has also trickled its way into the teen world. In fact, any forty-five year old pedophile can instantly transform into a twelve-year old by tapping into a teen chat room, typing in twelve-year old lingo, and pushing send. An unsuspecting preteen or teen could very well offer his or her information to this sick individual and end up cut into pieces under someone's porch.

The part where global communication has been enhanced is certainly a good thing, but there are aspects to this kind of connection that can fall into a frightening category. Much of the danger with the Internet, even for adults is that it doesn't always seem as *real* as it is, much like purchasing something with a credit card doesn't feel as *real* as handing over cash. Underneath it all we know that when we use a credit card that the item isn't free, but it can feel that way. In fact, we may not have bought that same item if we had to reach into our pocket and then feel the cash leave our fingertips. We may have thought things over a little more thoroughly. So it is with the Internet. We are staring into a screen, typing something to a person that we can't see. It doesn't feel as real as if we were standing face to face. It doesn't even feel as real as writing a letter the old-fashioned way, as there are so many more steps involved. When a person writes a letter, they are normally focused on the person they are writing to, as well as conscious of putting something in writing. Then, unless you have a supply of stamps in a desk drawer, there is a trip to the post office, as well as a conscious awareness of dropping the letter into the mailbox, knowing that once it is mailed that there is no turning back. The person on the receiving end will get something in writing with the signature of the person who wrote it.

Just as when television first came out, there was a certain period where only a select few on the block were able to afford them. Then after a while the prices dropped and before long everyone in middle-America had a television set. As far as personal computers are concerned, we are now past this stage, in that most homes in middle-America have *at least* one, and many of our preteens and teens have computers in their bedrooms. These kids, for better or worse, have access to the world. Having an e-mail pal in Ireland can be a very cool, cultural experience, but unfortunately this is not what many teens are doing with this very adult privilege.

Just as some teens are on a search and destroy mission in other areas, romancing risk at every given chance, so it is with the Internet. What makes the Internet so vulnerable to abuse is the obvious anonymity, as well as the lack of *realness* or *permanence* of the message sending. Teen bullies, especially, are enjoying this new avenue to torment their victims. They can say far more in cyber-space to completely destroy a classmate's self esteem than they ever could in person because it is far more difficult to be caught. They do not have to take accountability for their actions and cruelty, which makes the Internet a feeding frenzy for cyber-cowards.

According to Amy Harmon, author of *Internet Gives Teenage Bullies Weapons to Wound From Afar,* "The technology, which allows its users to inflict pain without being forced to see its effect, also seems to incite a deeper level of meanness. Psychologists say the distance between bully and victim on the Internet is leading to an unprecedented-and often unintentional-degree of brutality, especially when combined with a typical adolescent's lack of impulse control and under developed empathy skills." Parry Aftab, executive director of WiredSafety.org, a non-profit group that has been fielding a growing number of calls from parents and school administrators worried about bullying says that, "We're always talking about protecting kids on the internet from adults and bad people," and that, "We forget that we sometimes need to protect kids from kids."

Harmon continues to explain that, "For many teenagers. Online harassment has become a part of everyday life. But schools, which tend to focus on problems that arise on their property, and parents, who tend to assume that their children know better than they do when it comes to computers, have long overlooked it. Only recently has it become pervasive enough that even the adults have started paying attention." Harmon continues to discuss that many schools have been dealing with the broad spectrum of teenage aggression, including physical bullying and sexual harassment, and that one school psychologist, Susan Yuratovac, from Hilltop Elementary School in Beachwood, Ohio, will be "devising a new curriculum to address the shift to electronic daunting." Ms. Yuratovic says that she has, "kids coming into school upset daily because of what happened on the Internet the night before." Ms. Yuratovac says she hears things from the kids such as "We were online last night and somebody said I was fat," or "They asked me why I wear the same pair of jeans every day, or "They say I have Wal-Mart clothes."

Sexually speaking, Harmon states that counselors say, "Boys make more explicit sexual comments online than off." Comments are made regarding body image, and in some cases digital pictures and videos are dispersed through cyberspace for any and all to see. Harmon discusses an incident involving an eighth-grade girl at Horace Mann School in the Riverdale section of the Bronx sending "a digital photo of herself masturbating to a male classmate on whom she had a crush," and that, "it quickly appeared on a file sharing network that teenagers use to trade music. Hundreds of New York private school students saw the video, in which the girl's face was clearly visible, and it was available to a worldwide audience of millions." Not only that, Harmon continues, one student from another school commented that "students could go online at school while the girl was there and watch it." There have been many incidents such as this one in schools across the country where pictures, videos, or cruel messages were widely dispersed with purely cruel intentions. But, Harmon says, "a growing number of teenagers are learning the hard way that words sent into cyberspace can have more severe consequences than a telephone conversation or a whispered confidence. As ephemeral as they seem, instant messages (better known as I.M.'s) form a written record often wielded as a potent weapon for adolescent betrayal and torment."

The Internet has also opened the door for teens to escape into a world where they can be social *safely*. For a teen with a social disorder, or who is just shy, this is a very bad thing as they will be enabled by their computer to feel as if they are developing relationships without actually doing so. There is little if any fear of rejection, which is the key motivator in cyber-relationships. Their minds are tricked into thinking that they have accomplished that which terrifies them, to interact or engage with another person. For teens, or adults for that matter, the Internet can create a delusional sense of human connection. This *feeling* of being connected is false, and the longer it continues this sense of falseness will fade and the teen will begin to feel that she does in fact have friends. He may begin to believe that he is dating someone even though he has never actually had a face to face conversation with this person.

The other key motivator for cyber-relationships is the convenience. Teens or adults who are socially lazy can carry on lengthy conversations on their own schedules without ever leaving the comfort of their living rooms. There is no need to get dressed up, to pay attention to or respond to body language, and there is no money to be spent. There is no driving involved. There is no risk that the date may go on for longer than planned when you had your mind set on watching Seinfeld reruns when you got home. Basically, cyber-relationships have little effort involved, and since a person always has the choice to *log off* on the spot, there is a certain delusion of having control at all times which is encouraged also. In real-life relationships, it is not always easy to simply *log off*, or it least it shouldn't be.

For teens especially, this form of *anti-social* socializing is particularly unhealthy and developmentally dangerous. As most of us are aware, each developmental life stage has a purpose. Infants need to attach and bond. By doing so, they develop a sense of internal security that they will carry with them throughout their lives. By not doing so, they will struggle with relationships and be challenged to acquire and maintain a positive sense of self. The job of a toddler is to become autonomous. This is the stage of individuation where they separate and begin to realize on some level that they are a different self than their mother and father. They discover free will, which is evident by the toddler's very typical love of the word *no*. The adventurous toddler will challenge external limits in order to figure out their internal boundaries and reify their sense of internal security as Mom or Dad chases after them and brings them back safely. Early childhood and tween-hood, depending on which psychologist or theories you are a fan of, have a lot to do with concrete thinking and the ability to reason. Adolescence, the life stage where an individual makes the transition from childhood to adulthood, is where abstract thinking begins to take place and is also the age where kids begin to more actively socialize and date.

This is the life stage where the lessons have to do with the quest for self-awareness and purpose, as well as what it means to be male or female. Teens learn through trial and error how to relate with peers as well as the opposite gender. Homosexual teens may be beginning to have their first thoughts, feelings, and dreams about the same gender. The Internet is the perfect hideout for a gay teen who does not want to come to terms with his or her sexual orientation. It is also a convenient place to stay beneath the radar for a heterosexual teen who is relationship phobic. These teens will eventually leave this life stage and enter adulthood without learning the life lesson of this developmental period. They may escape the pain of adolescence to some degree, however, their emotional growth will be stunted in a sense, resulting in a chronological adult with underdeveloped coping skills who is emotionally inept. It is normal for adolescents to have these fears, however, far fewer teens in the pre-computer days would have been enabled to hide out for so long. For better or worse, the world around them would have forced them to interact to some degree which would have them in a much better place as adults.

Sexually speaking, those embarrassing moments that most of us would rather leave in the closet with the rest of our skeletons, where our sexual curiosity was expressed via such games as post office and spin the bottle, have given way to sexually explicit pictures and videos. For many millennial teens this is more information than they want or can handle, but it is difficult to turn it off. There is pressure to be sexual and to be interested in all that is sexual, ready or not. In fact, I remember being a preteen and getting my information indirectly through my best friend's older cousin. It was a bit fragmented and uncertain, so we used our imagination as we tried not to grimace as she told us. There were no digital photos or videos, only her stories, which lacked any real detail. I also remember this being enough information for my friend and me. We would go off on our own and process it all up in a tree or on top of our clubhouse. Then life would return to normal until the next visit from the fourteen-year old sex guru. When I think about what we would have been thinking and feeling had we witnessed a digital video of a girl our own age masturbating or two people having intercourse, I am honestly not sure that I would have an answer. The information we got back in 1979 from a teenager was enough. We talked; we giggled, then went back up in the tree fort.

Because of teens having access to the Internet, and therefore access to the adult world regardless of how sick or inappropriate, *normal* adolescent sexual exploration has changed. What has also changed, is the ability for sex addiction to occur earlier and more frequently than it would without the Internet. There are more and more kids left unsupervised across the country. As mentioned previously, many of these computers are in the sanctity of the teen bedroom where a quick tap on the keyboard can make an unwanted screen disappear in an instant when the teen-radar picks up on parental footsteps coming down the hallway. There are also millions of rural teens that do not have the opportunities or activities that are available to the teens in the burbs. Teens who live in remote areas where they lack shopping malls, ice-rinks, or movie theatres may be more apt to plug into the computer. From the opposite perspective, inner-city teens may be overwhelmed with their world of metal detectors, gangs, drug dealers, and subway anxiety. They may enjoy the security of socializing safely in their bedrooms. Regardless of the reason, too much time spent on the computer is a bad thing, and as is true with anything else, behaviors can become habits. Looking up porn on the internet and masturbating can be easier than learning how to interact with the opposite gender.

Habits, of course, are all about the *pay-off*. If we continue to do behaviors that make us feel good on some level, whether or not they are healthy, they will become habits and habits as we all know are difficult to break. There is also the notion that some kids are going to be more pre-disposed to addiction than others for genetic as well as environmental reasons. I don't believe anyone disputes at this point that a child with at least one alcoholic parent has an increased chance of becoming an alcoholic herself. It is also known that addictions can be substituted. In other words, the adult child of an alcoholic may have been very careful as far as monitoring his alcohol intake, but then later in life may find himself struggling with a gambling problem, or his sister with over-spending. This scenario is not different with sex, time spent staring at a screen, work, or physical exercise. If the behavior is affecting the life of your teen in a negative way, preventing his happiness, growth, and ability to interact positively with his family and friends than he may need help. Certainly, if he is searching out porn on the Internet anyway he is in need of the time and attention of a parent, but especially if he is unable to control his behavior and being deceptive about his *private* life, it is very much time to step in.

15

Teens and Social Disorders

Being a teen is certainly challenging enough without adding a twenty-pound weight to your back. In the teen world, this could qualify as one of the toughest *extra* things to deal with, as this is the time for social growth and social pretty much everything. This is the time of life when a teen wakes up worrying about what to wear, how her hair looks, what brand his sneakers are, and what will happen if he doesn't make the football team. She worries about being thin enough, and *he* may worry about being thin enough, not to mention muscle size and tone. Teens feel that all eyes are on them, and their entire day revolves around fitting in and being part of a group. They worry whether or not they will be invited to so and so's party next weekend, as everybody who is anybody will be there. They think about will happen if they are not invited, and what they will say at lunch in the cafeteria when everyone else is talking about it. For most teens, their biggest fear is being left out, but this is different. Socially anxious teens worry about being left out *and* they worry about being included, as being social and interacting with peers all day long takes everything they have in them.

So then, where does this leave a teen with social anxiety, autism, or Aspergers syndrome? These teens' biggest fear is like a double-edged sword. They are afraid of being left out *and* they are afraid of being invited also. In fact, I once worked with a tween who was very bright, and very artistic, who struggled socially. Her parents reported that she wasn't comfortable being touched and didn't ever pursue affection with them. When they would try to grab a quick hug from her, she would not resist in a defiant way, but would stiffen up like a board. When they thought back to her infancy, they agreed that she had never been a *snuggly* baby. She was, however, very content. Her parents said that she rarely cried and enjoyed just sitting and taking it all in. They found this upsetting early on and then realized that it wasn't anything they were doing, but simply how their daughter was *wired*.

These are some of the classic signs of autism, now labeled Asperger's Syndrome if the symptoms are mild which with this particular child they were. She got good grades in school and was a brilliant artist, yet going to school all day long would literally drain the life right out of her. Her parents reported that she would come home after school and talk in detail (in the monotone story-telling voice so characteristic of kids with Asperger's Syndrome) about what went on during recess and it would sound as if she was involved in the game or conversation. During a meeting with her teachers, the parents were informed that their daughter was walking back and forth on the side of the playground *watching* everything that was going on. They were told that she hadn't ever participated in a game with the other kids. Her father told me that the first thing she did when she got off the bus was to go straight to her dog, who she readily gave affection to, then to the swings. The motion of the swings would ease the overwhelming anxiety that had accumulated throughout her day.

For this young girl, being *up* and *on* all day took everything she had in her just to survive. In fact, her father had mentioned to me early on that one of their concerns was how to get their daughter to the point of being able to feel secure enough socially to raise her hand to go to the bathroom. Up until that point she wouldn't go to the restroom all day to the point where she would get a stomach-ache. They also reported, that it wasn't until she reached the second grade that she felt comfortable eating lunch in front of the other kids. She would just sit there quietly, then eat some of her lunch on the bus ride home.

In addition to these symptoms, probably one of the toughest things for this tween to deal with, was change. Her parents reported that she had always been very neat and orderly. She had always gotten up at the same time, 5:00 am, since they could remember. At this early hour, their daughter would quietly make her bed and clean her room. Everything had a place, and she couldn't rest easy until she made sure that her possessions were in their rightful positions on her shelf and desk. She also needed to know in advance if anything was going to change in her schedule, or they could expect an anxiety melt down. Even something such as where her family was going for Thanksgiving, was news that needed to be delivered weeks in advance. This socially anxious tween needed to know what was in her future as she did not handle surprises well. As far as changes in school, her parents learned to brace themselves for the transitions between vacations as well as the changes in teachers from grade to grade.

In working with this HFA (high functioning children with Asperger's) tween, one of the most challenging aspects of the treatment process was witnessing the guilt her parents felt. Her mother felt guilty for not realizing her daughter's challenges sooner. She told me that by the time her daughter was about three years old she knew that something was different, but she couldn't quite put her finger on it. She explained that her daughter was high functioning in every other way, so it didn't occur to her to have her daughter evaluated. Her mother said that she seemed extremely shy and timid, and thought that she would just have to work with her daughter to get her to be more engaging.

According to www.Asbergerssyndrome.net, this is not uncommon, as many HFA "children's social problems are not recognized until they enter preschool. The first things noticed may be a tendency to avoid spontaneous social interactions, to having problems maintaining a conversation, and to have a tendency to repeat phrases and make odd statements. They do not make many friends easily and often have difficulty keeping them. Emotional responses such as anger, aggression, or anxiety may be excessive or inappropriate to the situation. HFA children also prefer a set routine to frequent changes in the environment." In addition, "Adolescence may bring crisis for HFA children because the very social skills they lack are central to adolescent social development." He further explains that "the common application of social skills training for Asperger's children is based on a core misunderstanding of why HFA children do not demonstrate good social skills. The problem is more of one being able to access skills than not having them." This becomes apparent when an Asperger's kid is observed doing fine socially interacting with the adults in his or her life. If they simply did not have the tools, then they obviously would be unable to engage with adults also. Some theorize that this may be do to the Aspergers child not having the omnipresent fear of rejection with adults that they do with their peers.

A further misconception that people have with Aspergers' kids is that they can help them by *throwing them into the fire*, so to speak. He further explains that, "skilled social interaction is not a thought out, planned interaction. It is the brainstem's reflexive responding to another person, like dancing. Social skills training is generally ineffective and can actually confound social permanence because it teaches cognitively guided, planned, social interaction. This shifts the Asperger's child away from doing the reflexive social dance." In fact, he continues, "Each time they are forced into social situations by well meaning helpers, the more negative social conditioning may occur. This sets up more negative experiences which can make things worse, not better. It does no good to push these children into socialization experiences if they are not going to be positive."

With the Asperger's children I have worked with, what I have found to be highly successful is to work with the parents to do *supportive socializing* with their child. What this means, is to arrange one on one play dates when the child is younger, not too frequently and with lots of notice so they are able to adjust to the change in their daily routine. After a while, the child does get more socially comfortable and somewhat desensitized to both the fear and pressure of being social. It is certainly important not to force things, but I have found that parents getting kids started with a game or suggesting an activity can bridge the social gap for the Asperger's child. Sometimes all they need is their hand held while they do what they fear most, interacting with a peer. Of course this only holds true if the experience is a positive one. With this particular young girl I worked with, her social treatment plan was highly effective. Her mother paired her up with a same gender playmate once a week for several years until the child became comfortable. It also helps to have a child over who is *low-maintenance* for the Aspergers child, as they can get overwhelmed with a child who has a high energy level and is easily distracted.

After the child's comfort level has increased, it is important to stay on top of not sliding backwards. It takes the Aspergers child all they have in them to increase their social comfort level, so it is extremely important not to jeopardize their progress by allowing them to be in a situation which could be overwhelming and thereby undermine their progress. It is therefore usually a good idea to avoid sleepovers until these children are almost *over-ready* to take them on, as it is simply too long for an Asperger's kid to hold it together. They will most likely not say a word, have the life drained out of them, then come home and fall apart. Therefore, parents of an Asperger's child really need to be on top of their game when it comes to his or her play-dates and social engagements. As these children become teenagers, they will of course appreciate having more choices just as any other teen would. However, the parent of the Asperger's child will still need to micro-manage a little longer, in order to protect his or her self-esteem as well as to keep their child in an emotionally safe place, free of any additional anxiety.

Most experts would also agree that if a child is unable to express himself in the traditional manner, that another avenue must be found as a vehicle to release his emotions, an alternative outlet. For many, the answer is art. Art therapy has been utilized by many clinicians working with children with Autism, Asperger's, Post Traumatic Stress Syndrome, as well as many other conditions, illnesses, and mood disorders that prevent a child from being able to freely express herself. Art serves as an alternative route, or detour around the emotional road block, where a child can find his or her own way of making how they feel be known to those on the outside. It serves as a link between the very private inner world of these kids, with the overwhelming outside world. For many of them, art can be liberating as it sets them free from isolation and loneliness, as well as the feelings of sadness and hopelessness that often accompany their repeated failed attempts to communicate and conform with the outer world. Unlike the more familiar corrective responses these kids have become used to, Art can't be wrong. It can only be unique and colorful just as they are.

16

Teens, Parents, and ADD

I felt a Cleaving in my Mind-
As if my brain had split-
I tried to match it-Seam by Seam-
But could not make them fit.

The thought behind, I strove to join
Unto the thought before-
But Sequence raveled out of Sound-
Like balls-upon a Floor.

—Emily Dickson (1864)

Your teen is fidgety, restless, or she spends the majority of her classroom time staring out the window. He is forgetful, easily distracted, and appears to have very little impulse control regardless of the consequences you give him. You have had more conversations with teachers, coaches, and counselors than you would care to count. In fact, the parenting skills and strategies that you used on your other kids, that were for the most part successful, don't seem to work on this one. She is different.

As a parent, you are frustrated because things should be easier by now and they are not. He is still *high maintenance* and now you have the additional fears and worries that accompany poor impulse control, especially with drugs and alcohol. Certainly all teens are at risk for unprotected sex, drugs, and alcohol, as well as other dangerous behaviors, however, for the teen with ADD the risk is even higher. These teens have even *less* of an ability to think things through and to see around the corner from their actions. The ADD teen is present moment oriented, and for the most part cares only about what is going on right here and right now. They are fun and spontaneous, and often very popular, as they like to attract attention and perform for their friends. Of course, this is all well and good until the performance involves something inappropriate or unacceptable and you get a call (or numerous calls) from his school.

This is where the *negative* comes in, and for the ADD teen there is more negative than just about anything else in his or her life. In fact, more than likely, it has been this way since he can remember and he has probably become used to it. This is a very bad thing, as the primary casualty of hearing constant negative about oneself is obviously self-esteem. Everything else, such as reading ability and comprehension, tools to handle frustration and manage distraction, will fall into place along with guidance and consistent effort. What will *not* automatically improve, however, and may actually take years to heal, is the ADD teen's self esteem.

When she hears and internalizes daily messages from *her people* about all that she is not doing right, her spirit is being damaged. Rarely does a day go by for the ADD teen that she does not have at least one moment of feeling like a failure, and most days there are lots of moments. She is already aware on some level that she is different, and she questions herself constantly as far as what she should or shouldn't have said, or what she could have done better.

Her mind is on fast-forward, and she spends much of her day filtering out the volumes of incoming messages that she receives. She doesn't want to miss the important ones, but doesn't need the unimportant ones. The ADD teen has to regulate the thoughts that she is bombarded with all day long, especially during quiet moments such as when she is reading or taking a test. She can be halfway through a page in English class when all of the sudden she starts to wonder who will be going out for the soccer team next week, what is on the lunch menu for today, what chores she'll have to do when she gets home, and who might ask her to the dance on Friday. When she tunes back in, she realizes that the class is almost over and the bell is about to ring. She realizes that she didn't take too many notes. Anxiety sets in because there is a test next week and she caught only fragments of what is going on. She wonders if she should ask a friend if she can look at her notes, but then figures that maybe she shouldn't ask because that would be like copying homework and she doesn't want anyone to be upset with her. Oh well, there is always tomorrow.

As far as school related issues, in addition to the daydreaming element of ADD, which results in a persistent underlying anxiety created by the fear of what was missed in class, there are also the elements of forgetfulness, an overall lack of organizational skills, and difficulty managing time. The locker or backpack of an ADD teen is normally the equivalent of a small natural disaster. At any given moment the door could bust open causing an avalanche of papers and six-month-old banana peels. This is true of most teens to some degree, but for the ADD teen it is much worse. Their complete mental disorganization is exemplified by the atmosphere which they create for themselves on the *outside*. The clutter and chaos causes them to be even more distracted and further impairs their ability to function in the classroom setting. Organization, or lack there of, should not be overlooked by parents, as this can make or break your child's success in school. By helping her to minimize her external chaos, you will minimize her internal chaos as well. This can be a very liberating and empowering feeling. This sets the ADD teen up to succeed, and they need this support. It is also important for the parent of the ADD teen to know that it is all right to help your ADD teen a little more than you would a teen without ADD. It is more important that they have the tools they need to manage their day than it is to prove a point or make a parental stand. This is not enabling them. This is what it takes for the ADD teen to survive and to feel good about himself.

It is also important for parents to know that it is never too late. Just as with anything else, parents can re-evaluate how things are going with their child. They can consciously determine what seems to be working and what seems to be creating friction and resistance. Colleen Alexander-Roberts writes in *ADHD And Teens*, that though "parents do not cause the primary symptoms of ADHD," that, "the way parents handle misbehavior, disrespectful behavior, rebellious acts, confrontations, deviance, and even day-to-day mistakes can make their life with a teen with ADHD either one of harmony or one of discord. Parents who seem to be always clashing with their teenagers need to stop and evaluate their parenting skills." Colleen Alexander-Roberts further explains, that parents "must also be willing to make a strong commitment to change. The way a parent responds to problematic behavior, their expectations, the teen's temperament, and how she reacts to your parenting methods are all factors that need to be examined. Obviously, if parents want to see changes made in the home and with their teens, they must be willing to make changes within themselves."

To begin with, all teens need limits, and this is even more so for the teen with ADD. She needs to know what the rules are and what the consequences will be if they are broken. She needs clarity. Colleen Alexander-Roberts explains that, "Teens want and need limits, even if they object to them. Boundaries permit them to explore and challenge the rules-a task of normal development-and learn that their parents care about them and their actions." She also explains that along with the "firm" part there needs to be a "loving" part as a purely dominating approach where blind obedience is expected, will not work. At this stage of the game, where your ADD teen is striving towards adulthood, he or she will benefit from some explanation on occasion. It doesn't mean to *bend*, just to explain, especially if it is an issue of physical or emotional safety. The ADD Teen needs to know which rules are flexible and which are *not*. Alexander-Roberts states that, "Teens are more apt to abide by the rules if they have been given the opportunity to help establish the rules. Firm and loving parents also provide unconditional love, support, and spend focused time with their teenagers. They recognize that their teens are emerging adults with developmental tasks that need to be experienced and explored, and they actively encourage them to seek independence, make choices and decisions, and accept responsibility. Teenagers of firm and loving parents naturally feel more secure, loved, and have higher self-esteem."

Another area that parents may need to work through with their ADD teen is his or her *hypersensitivity*. The teen that struggles with ADD is hypersensitive to her surroundings, which can cause her to internalize and react to much of what is said to her. The ADD teen is similar to a nerve without the protective myelin sheath, the fatty layer that keeps it from being constantly stimulated. These teens are exposed nerves that are like catchers' mitts for all incoming information. It is difficult for them to sort it out as well as to gage the relative importance of what they are hearing and feeling, which is why the ADD teen is prone to overreacting. He often cannot tell what is huge from what is no big deal, and may react to both incidents with the same degree of intensity, especially if he was already worked up and frustrated to begin with. ADD teens frequently get caught up in the momentum of a situation, and once they pick up speed it can be extremely difficult for them to slow themselves down. This is often when an explosion occurs, as the ADD teen at this point, basically cannot get out of his own way.

What is important for parents to know about the hypersensitivity element of their teen is that they cannot change it. Right, wrong, or indifferent, this is how your child is wired, and probably will be forever. Where parents can help and make a difference for their child, is to teach them how to manage their lives in such a way as to prevent this momentum from picking up to begin with. Just as with most other areas of damage control, prevention is the best medicine. Teaching your teen to make *conscious* decisions and choices is a sure way to limit these short-circuiting moments and explosive outbursts, as it is *passive* thinking and reacting that so frequently causes the ADD kid to get into trouble. They need to be taught how to take the offensive approach and limit the information coming in, and to limit their obligations and commitments. They need to be taught how to say *no*. Just as an alcoholic needs to make sobriety a priority, so it is with the ADD teen and their much needed *down time*. Without this quiet time to get re-centered, they will be headed for self-destruction at full speed.

Lynn Weiss, Ph.D., writes in *Give Your ADD Teen a Chance*, that "Because your ADD teen is so sensitive, he feels everything that goes on around him, including your feelings, wishes and desires. When your teen's hypersensitivity sets him up to make commitments he can't live up to, your job is to help him learn to be responsible and truthful, or to reap the consequences of not staying in control of himself." Weiss describes some strategies that may help your ADD teen understand his hypersensitivity, which is the first step towards empowering him emotionally. These kids need to be taught how to be in the *driver's seat*. She begins by suggesting that parents build their ADD teen's unique ability to sense what "others may feel or want." This is certainly a good place to put a positive spin on things and to build up the teen's ability to be intuitive of *her people* and of her surroundings, and of course, that she cares so deeply for others, as this is a highly desirable character trait. We *want* our teens to be thinking and caring about others. Next, Weiss says it is a good idea for parents to, "Set limits on what you expect from your teen," and to explain to their ADD teen that they also need to be sensitive to their own wants and needs. The ADD teen needs to be taught the importance of taking responsibility for herself.

Weiss continues to explain that as parents we need to inform and educate our teens about how they are setting themselves up to fail when they take on too much. We need to explain that "When any of us commits to something another person wants but it's not good for us, we jeopardize our own well-being," and that in the end, "we let both ourselves and the other person down." She goes on to say that the ADD teen needs "permission to do what is best for him," and that he should be expected "to be honest about how he feels." This is where parents need to be on their toes and actively listening, so that when a situation does arise which may involve multi-tasking that they can assist their ADD teen in being proactive, and to filter out what it is that he truly wants and is capable of. Lastly, Weiss explains that parents need to have a plan and to be clear with their teen on what will happen if "he does not take responsibility for his hypersensitivity." Just as with any other behavior, parents need to impose limits, which serve as *walls* in a sense, for the teen to bounce off of. When they head in the wrong direction and bounce off a wall they learn that they cannot go that way and then try another route. This is all part of the learning process of self-awareness, as well as the process of *behavior shaping*, meaning the process by which our teens learn which behaviors will be deemed appropriate and acceptable, and which will not.

For those who are young adults with ADD, things can be challenging at times also. I remember that it wasn't until I was a sophomore in college that I figured out the label for my symptoms and difficulties. I knew that I daydreamed a lot, and that it was difficult to read. In fact, I could get through about ten or fifteen pages without it taking an enormous amount of effort. Half way through a chapter I would disappear into the world of the college co-ed. Though my eyes would be reading the words, my mind was somewhere else, off in a distant land. When I would "snap out of it", I realized that I had to go back and re-read it all.

As an ADD young adult, I struggled to manage my time, especially at college where there is so much to do and so many new friends to make. In fact, the campus post office was right across the parking lot from my dorm, and it used to take me roughly two hours to go and check my mailbox. There were so many people to chat with on the way there and back. The snack bar was there too, as well as the college store. Thankfully, our cross-country coach made the whole team take a time-management class when we were freshmen or I would have been up a creak without both paddles, or the boat for that matter. The two-hour mandatory class was held at the college's student resource center. They gave us a stack of blank schedules for us to fill in for each day of the week. Since I had to sit there anyway, I filled it out. I had never done anything like this before. Just to see my schedule in front of me in writing reduced my anxiety. Too bad there was nothing like this at my high school. It would have helped a lot.

As far as the over-stimulation factor, running was my outlet. Without it, I would have gone off the deep end, though I don't think it was anything I was aware of consciously. Not yet anyway. I was doing what I needed to do to survive. There was so much going on around me. As I was a very fun-loving ADD young adult, it was nearly impossible for me to say no to any of it. *No* was a word that was not in my vocabulary. If I was invited, I went. I didn't want to miss anything. Eventually, when I would *hit the wall*, so to speak, my brain would short-circuit. I would then hop into my little yellow (very old) Volkswagen Rabbit, and disappear for an afternoon without telling anybody. I would drive to Stowe by myself and get a soda at the Country Store, then turn around and come back. Just being in the car alone for that short time, re-charged my batteries. I was managing my ADD without being aware of it. All I knew was that if I didn't make the break to be alone for two hours that my head would explode. I think that during my entire stay as an undergraduate, I slept for a combined five hours, total.

As a parent with ADD, there have been challenging moments for me also. Of course by now, I am aware that I am wired differently than other people, and far more aware of what I need to do to mange my ADD and my day. Managing my day is very important, as my ADD doesn't go away. Some days are more challenging than others, but it is always there and I need to stay on top of it in order to be a loving and affective parent. I need to be able to recognize when I am taking on too much and slow things down. This is probably the most difficult area for me to manage, as multi-tasking is pretty standard for a mother of five, and to be truthful, I can handle quite a few balls in the air at once. However, it is important for me to know and to be able to recognize my own personal limits. What I can handle may be different from what another parent can handle, and I need to remind myself that I need not compare myself to anyone else. When I manage my ADD effectively, all is smooth and harmonious with the family. When things slip past me, and I find myself in a frenzied blur, well, this is where Mom can get a little snippy. This is the situation we try to avoid.

At no time is it easier to slip into *autopilot* than during the holiday season. As far as over-stimulation, the festivities around us tend to take on a life of their own. The cookie-baking, gift buying, wrapping, card sending, and school concerts pick up momentum with great speed, much like a snowball gets bigger and faster as it rolls down hill. After bouncing off numerous walls at nearly forty years of age, I have finally found what works for our family. What works is to keep it simple. We no longer have a huge breakfast on Christmas morning, as it was too difficult to try and run back and forth between rooms to watch the kids open their presents. Now we wait and have a more continental breakfast of fruit and banana bread, which I prepare a couple of days before. Then, on the most over-stimulating day of the year, I can just pull them out of the fridge, sit on the couch, and take it all in. We have our big fancy celebration on Christmas Eve which works out much better.

ADD parents have it tougher being parents in today's world the rest of the year as well, as times have changed. Back in the 70's when I grew up, nobody drove their kids all over the place for Tae Kwon Do or ballet. We had the backyard. That's it. Our friends were comprised of who lived within biking distance. We didn't get driven to anyone's house to play, and we didn't even go home on anyone else's bus, at least not for a regular day of playing. If we went to school with a note to go home with little so and so, it was usually because your younger sibling was getting her tonsils out or something. It isn't this way anymore. Parents run themselves into the ground, driving their kids all over the place, teaching them that being over-scheduled, running, and doing is a good way to be. It my opinion, it is tragic, as it represents the loss of childhood.

There is a lot to be said for just hanging out in the backyard. The ADD parent, who wakes up feeling fast on the inside has even more to contend with in today's society just to keep up with it all. This is especially true if the ADD parent lives in the suburbs where all that people are doing is sort of right in her face, as well as in the faces of her kids. It took me a while, but at my seasoned age of forty, I have given myself permission to step out of the twister of busy-ness and watch it go by. Our kids each have their *thing* that they are into. In the fall it is soccer for two of them. In the spring it is baseball. My oldest daughter is into her artwork and studying French. They have made choices. When we are running around like anxious gazelles, this is what we are role-modeling for our children. We are teaching them that we need to do and spend to be happy. To sit still with our thoughts, our feelings, and ourselves becomes an impossibility. We need to ask ourselves if this is really what we want for our young children, our teens, or our young adults, because what they are seeing us do, they will eventually do also.

There are some very simple little tips to slow it all down such as not answering the phone during dinner. I remember thinking my mother was evil because I was shut off from my teenage world for an hour while we sat together and discussed the goings on of the day as a family. I grimaced over my plate for several years sticking mental pins in an imaginary miniature doll resembling my mother, wishing that she would go ruin someone else's life. It wasn't until I became a mother myself that I realized the importance of shutting the world out during this precious and valuable family time. Turning off the ringer on the phone conveys the message to your kids that they are more important than whoever it is who is trying to call. It shows them that you value what they have to say. And besides, the world will be there waiting after the dishes are done.

For the ADD parent, this is not only about preserving family time, but about reducing stimulation also, and for the ADD parent this is the primary objective. Too many signals in the air make things cloudy and chaotic, until there is no longer clearance to the tower at all. For the ADD parent, the message is, "I, too, can take care of myself. I can manage my ADD. I am in control." Even as adults, we need little mental reminders now and again to boost our own self-esteem. I know that for myself, when my external atmosphere gets out of control, and I find myself making passive choices by not acting consciously, that I do not feel very good about myself. As grown-ups, we want and need to be in control. Certainly I do not mean to insinuate that we need to be control freaks, micro-managing every minute detail, but simply to have a grip on ourselves, and our family relationships. We can do this by limiting the information coming in, as well as our commitments. ADD moms, especially, are champions at multi-tasking, however, even we have our limits and we need to know them. It is when we fall asleep at the wheel that we have problems.

If it happens that things do slip away from us, we need to be able to recognize that momentum is picking up and take a time out, even if we have to excuse ourselves to head for the bathroom for five minutes to collect our thoughts and get centered. Taking a few minutes to get a grip is better than ripping someone's face off, which hopefully at this point your family understands. Another tip for short-circuit prevention is to stay consistently physically active. This tip actually falls under the *essential* category, as those of us with ADD can rarely focus if we have been sedentary for too long. As the mother of five, I rarely have much free time to go off on my own. In fact, as it is, I get up at 5:00 am to write. What I do to manage the physical needs created by my ADD is to do things with my kids. We ski and snow-shoe in the winter, and we swim and take walks in the summer. We don't always go for long. Sometimes the walk is around picking wild flowers, but we are outside and moving which is enough.

Another tip which falls under the *essential* category is time spent alone in solitude. As I just mentioned, as a mom of five, I need to carve out time for myself as we are an active family committed to spending time with and interacting with our kids. This may sound like a simple task, but is actually one of the most challenging. There is always something else we could be doing, always some pull on us as we try to sneak out the door. In fact, for me, this is my Achilles heal, as I am unable to present my best self to my family or the world without out this valuable time to get centered. It is not a lot of time. Sometimes after I write in the early morning I will head out for a short walk. Sometimes if I am pressed for time I will turn around at our neighbor's house down the road. This loop is only about fifteen minutes, but fifteen minutes spent the right way can do wonders. I return centered and focused, and my day is off to a good start.

Something else that helps me greatly is to limit my caffeine intake. This may not make sense to some as caffeine is a stimulant, the essence of the medications prescribed to treat ADD. For some reason, however, at least with adults, the affect is not the same. Caffeine makes an already racy mind even racier. I have one cup of coffee in the morning and rarely have a caffeinated soda in the afternoon unless I have a head cold or for some reason did not have a good night's sleep. Any more than this, and I may as well prepare for a distracted, unfocused, and edgy day.

Lastly, it is good to communicate to those around you when you are having an ADD day. Hopefully by now you have disclosed how you are wired with those you love and live with. If not, we need to go back to step one and start there, because *your people* need to know that you are different than they are, with different needs and different ways of doing things. I am very fortunate to have a wonderfully loving and supportive husband who does *get it* when I am having an ADD day and will give me the space that I need. It is important for us to communicate what it is that our needs are. As is true with anyone's issues, people for the most part are not mind-readers and will benefit from communication and the knowledge of what is going on. People being made aware that you are feeling over-stimulated and that you would appreciate it if they turned off the television for a little while, is better than snapping at them over something trivial when they have absolutely no idea what is going on inside of your head.

Just as you would do for your ADD teen, it is helpful if you provide yourself with structure, especially if you are a stay-at-home mom or dad. The ADD parent needs sustenance to his or her day, and if it is not there, then you must create it.

You must parent yourself by making small do-able lists so that you feel a sense of accomplishment and daily success. The "do-able" part is extremely important, as you do not want to set yourself up to fail. This is an all too common feeling for ADD people, to feel that they just can't get it together or that they are not grown-up on the inside even though their chronological age may not reflect that. We often feel inadequate next to our seemingly mature adult peers who have an easier time delaying gratification and managing impulse control than we do. If you have a partner, it is a good idea to have him or her manage the finances as this is usually not a strength for *our kind*. I can honestly say that I still have occasional moments where I feel this way also, that I still can't get it together, even after raising five beautiful children, being in a happy marriage of fifteen years, achieving a masters' degree in psychology, publishing two books and working on a third. It is part of the whole ADD thing, to feel that we are different, and it is because we are.

We lack the filter that other people have, and because of it we do not see things the way they do, but we see more. There is so much *focus*, ironically, on the struggles of the ADD individual and not as much *focus* on the strengths. Every single book that I have read on the subject, and I have read many, makes some mention of the uniqueness of the person with ADD. The ADD individual is usually very intelligent and has a creative eye that people can't quite explain. We just don't learn or express ourselves in *mainstream* ways. Since most of us have more energy than the Ever-Ready Bunny, we are usually lots of fun to be around. We are spontaneous and willing to try new things. Age does not seem to affect this, which is a good thing. While others slow down and play it safe, living a life of routine and early bird specials, the ADD adult will decide that her 60th birthday is the perfect time to try hot-air ballooning or skydiving. We are loving and passionate. There is nothing that we won't do for *our people*. And, by the way, there may be certain members of your family who don't get it. They may perceive your ADD as an excuse for what appears to them to be emotionally immature, impulsive, sometimes forgetful, disorganized, and/or reactive behavior. This is my suggestion.... ignore them and take a nice, long walk.

17

Sporadic Nurturing, Disconnection, and Teen Mental Illness

Extension of ourselves or moving out against the inertia of laziness we call work. Moving out in the face of fear we call courage. Love, then, is a form of work or a form of courage. Specifically, it is work or courage directed toward the nurture of our own or another's spiritual growth...Since it requires the extension of ourselves, love is always either work or courage. If an act is not one of work or courage, then it is not an act of love. There are no exceptions.

—M. Scott Peck, Ph.D.
Author of *The Road Less Traveled*

It isn't new news that teens are among the highest population at risk for depression and suicide. According to Maureen Empfield, M.D., and Nicholas Bakalar, authors of *Understanding Teenage Depression,* when they discuss the disease model of *clinical* depression state that, "some estimates are that as many as 8 percent of adolescents suffer from depression at some time during any one year period, making it much more common than, for example eating disorders, which seem to get more attention as a source of adolescent misery." They continue to explain that "clinical depression is not the same as a bad mood, or a feeling of unhappiness. It is a disease. Although there are some theories about it, no one knows exactly what causes depression in teenagers (or in anyone else, for that matter), but we do know that it is not caused by poor parenting, and that it cannot be cured by good parenting. Nor is it caused by the victim of the disease, something that for some people is all too easy to conclude. A "change in attitude" or a willingness on the part of the youngster to "straighten up and fly right" will not relieve the terrible symptoms of depression."

In addition, Empfield and Bakalar state that, "at the same time suicide among teenagers in the past fifteen years has grown by almost 25 percent, and among certain groups the rise is even higher. For example, black male adolescents, for reasons that are unclear, have seen a startling 146 percent increase in suicides in the same period." Depression is a complex and complicated disease, with physical, or organic components, as well as environmental or circumstantial components. I think most are aware that a teenager or adult can be genetically predisposed to the disease, but that it is not predetermined that a child will automatically become depressed because a parent or sibling has a history of depression. Being predisposed simply means that a child with a family history of depression may be at a higher risk of acquiring the disease than a child who has no history of depression or other related mental illness in his or her family.

In order to even begin to explore what would make a child want to end his or her life, we must first take a look at the intense feelings of despair and hopelessness behind this final action. We must look at the dynamic, or what it is that is really going on to cause such intense emotional pain that the child feels no way out but to take a chance on what is next. As previously discussed, *clinical depression* is a disease which has an organic base, and is frequently hereditary. There are other forms of depression, however, that may be the result of environmental circumstances as well as long-term, untreated anxiety. Some of the larger triggers may include divorce of the teen's parents, or the death of a family member or friend. For some, moving to a new geographic location can often result in an overwhelming loss for the teen as their peer groups are as necessary to them as bone marrow is to the rest of us. In fact, though many job transfers or planned moves cannot be helped, many parents drastically underestimate the affect it has on their preteen or teen. As there could not possibly be a worse time to uproot a child than middle school or high school, it is a good idea for parents to keep the lines of communication open and to brace themselves for an anger-fest.

As teens are on an emotional roller coaster to begin with, it therefore may not always take much to sink them into a mild to moderate depression. It can be something as small as a comment made by just the right person at just the wrong time in the hallway. For girls, and now unfortunately for many boys also, pretty much anything mentioned about body image, whether based in reality or coming from the depths of fabricated cruelty, can be enough to sink even the healthiest of teens into the dark abyss of low self worth. Anything involving rejection from the opposite gender will also do it, as the egocentric teen will interpret being turned down as equal to not being loved, wanted, or accepted by the world in general. In fact, most incoming messages for the teen tend to be global, another reason that they are at such a high risk for pretty much everything. For most of them, either all is well or all is not well, with very little gray area in between. Even with the disease model of clinical depression, which holds that a teenager can be physiologically predisposed to acquire the disease, so is it also true that a teen can be emotionally predisposed to acquiring the disease as well. This is where the issues of attachment and emotional disconnection come into play, as at the present moment, we are a very emotionally disconnected nation.

Many of our children have gradually become disconnected, and in order to reduce teen suicide and prevent further loss of young lives we need to take a good hard look at why. Of course, as explained, clinical depression is a physiological condition where the brain's chemistry is out of balance due to an ineffective or quantitative problem with dopamine, serotonin, or norepinephrine or with neurotransmitter uptake and release. Genuine, chemically based depression, however, in my opinion, is more of the exception and not what is going on with the majority of our nation's teens. Today's teenagers are very much an endangered species as they are not getting enough of what they truly need, enough of our time, love, and attention, and they are suffering because of it.

Similar to the way a two-year-old wanders off on the playground to explore and expand her world and sense of autonomy, so it is the same with the teen. The toddler looks back over her shoulder for the assurance that Mom or Dad is watching while they make this developmental leap, then wanders a few more feet and glances back again. When she goes one step too far, Mom calls her name then goes after her to bring her back. Unfortunately, all too often, the teen looks over his shoulder, hoping that someone is watching and finds that no one is there and that he is *out there* all alone. Though what our teens need from us as parents changes as they make the transition from child to adult, their most basic need to feel loved by us and connected to us does not change. How we maintain that connection may change, but our teens need to know that we are watching, even if from a comfortable and safe distance. They need to know that they are on a much longer leash, so to speak, than they had been when they were younger, but that they are still *tied* to us.

For such a large number of teens to be depressed in our country, something has gone radically wrong. I had the opportunity of speaking with Ms. Neila Anderson-Decelles, M.A., Clinical Supervisor of Turning Point, a day treatment center and alternative education program for children ages 6-18 who are primarily referred by the public school system for significant emotional and behavioral difficulties. Many of the kids also have incumbent learning challenges and a history of trauma. There is a certain percentage of kids who do not have a history of trauma or neglect, but who have been diagnosed with a variety of clinical disorders including Depression, Dystymia, Bipolar Disorder, Borderline Personality Disorder, Oppositional Defiant Disorder, and Conduct Disorder. The vast majority has experienced verbal, physical, and/or sexual abuse, and many have suffered from neglect.

At Turning Point, there are four classrooms, one for elementary children, one for middle school, one for junior high school kids, and one that would be considered a high school classroom. Ms. Anderson-Decelles explains that by the time a child gets to the Turning Point program that they have exhausted the public school system and most of the community resources. Ms. Anderson-Decelles adds that three-fourths of the students are male, and interestingly, all students currently attending the program who are between the ages of six and eleven are male. Around sixth grade girls begin to be referred to the program. Ms. Anderson-Decelles attributes this to the fact that many young girls who are victims of trauma or neglect do not tend to act out. She says, "they withdraw and become as invisible as possible," and that this feeling of wanting to be quieter and less noticeable, "tracks with the feeling of not wanting to be perpetrated upon. They get quieter and become less obvious, but then alongside these feelings is a lot of unattended anger and sadness. This causes many of these young girls to become self-injurious." Ms. Anderson-Decelles explains that they self-mutilate by cutting themselves in a variety of ways, and proceeds to explain something the girls refer to as a "woosie-fight." Ms. Anderson-Decelles describes a "woosie-fight" as a *game* that some of the kids engage in which involves, "taking an eraser and rubbing it on your arm as fast as you can until it bleeds. The one who gives up first by stopping to erase their skin, loses the game and earns the title of *woosie* or *pussy.*" Ms. Anderson-Decelles adds that, "it is exclusively our female students who are engaging in this behavior," and that she finds it upsetting because in addition to the obvious physical harm, that this behavior also "reinforces the dynamic of self-degradation so characteristic of adolescent females."

Lynn E. Ponton, M.D., writes in *The Romance of Risk-why teenagers do the things they do,* that "Self-mutilation occurs when teenagers injure their bodies on purpose, most commonly cutting or burning, and do not intend to kill themselves. It frequently begins in adolescence and can continue for decades if untreated. It is dangerous, with risks of permanent scarring, blood loss, infection (including HIV), and even death (by accidentally opening up a large vessel). Although a teen often begins by experimenting, often using his or her own body in an effort to end psychological pain, resolve a conflict, or even ostensibly, just to "see how it feels," it can evolve into a pattern, a habit, becoming one of the risk behaviors that is most difficult to stop. "Cutters," as they are known, carve words, pictures, and, most commonly, delicate slashes into arms, hands, legs, chest, face, stomach, or genitals using razors, knives, paper clips, bobby pins, pens, scissors, combs, pieces of glass, and fingernails. The teen who cuts often has experiences of depression or a history of sexual abuse. Self-mutilation is a part of a continuum of activities that involve scarification and the body; activities defined as "skin art," which can include branding, artistic scarring, body piercing, and tattooing, also fall along this continuum."

As issues regarding tattooing and body piercing have already been discussed in a previous chapter, we will simply reiterate that some adults view tattoos as a form of art and *some* adolescents are more superficially following a trend. For our purposes here, however, it is important to realize and evaluate what an adolescent's intentions are when they permanently alter themselves, as for most there is a statement being made or an emotion being expressed to someone, usually anger or pain. This anger is often directed toward the self, and the tattoo or piercing is the manifestation of self-hatred and a form of self-punishment. Most psychologists would agree that self-punishment is one of the most reinforcing dynamics of mental illness, as the *pay-off* is huge for the injured person, and therefore often becomes habitual, making it a very difficult behavior to substitute or stop. Ponton continues to explain that, "By many cutter's reports, the act of self-mutilation provides relief, albeit short-lived, from intense feelings of anxiety, anger, emptiness, and depression. Many who mutilate themselves also suffer from dissociation, a numbing defense common to victims of trauma, including sexual abuse. Dissociation is an altered state of consciousness, a feeling of being outside of one's body, of being unreal. It can be a way of "leaving" an unbearable situation, at least psychologically. Children who are being repeatedly sexually abused learn how to leave their painful reality and retreat into their own world. What works as a coping strategy during a traumatic event can become a habitual response to stress." Cutters often cut to *relieve* this psychological pain or as an attempt to emerge from a numb state of being in order to *feel*. Though body piercing and tattooing, as far as an *adolescent* is concerned, are not exactly the same, they are very much related. They are related because of the unifying dynamic of self-inflicted pain.

When Ms. Anderson-Decelles talks about this latest form of self-mutilation and the teens she works with at Turning Point she says, "We are hearing of young women piercing their nipples, their clitoris', and all kinds of body parts. Although, since it is socially condoned as being cool and sophisticated there are mentally healthy adolescents doing it also which skews the whole understanding of what self-mutilation is all about." Ms. Anderson-Decelles spoke of a conversation she had recently with an adolescent female who had just had her tongue pierced. The young girl was attempting to speak with a sore, thickened tongue to explain that her tongue didn't hurt. The young girl proudly showed Ms. Anderson-Decelles her newly pierced tongue, which she describes as "being swollen, bruised and scarred." Ms. Anderson-Decelles also found to be upsetting, "the fact that this young girl was attempting to convince me, through a thickened, bloody tongue, that it didn't hurt which just goes to show you how an adolescent can disassociate themselves from what they are doing to or with their bodies."

As far as the piercing of the female nipple, Ms. Decelles says that there is concern "for damage being done to the mammary glands as well as the emotional denial of the breast having anything to do with being nurturing." Even though the idea of the future and the potential for healthy motherhood is probably not on the forefront of most adolescent minds, on some level, there is an awareness of the body and an emotional connection to its reproductive role even if it is years ahead. Ms. Anderson-Decelles says that there may be some subconscious symbolism as far as forsaking motherhood by the mere fact that by piercing this particular body part, that the adolescent female "has no awareness of the breast being nurturing. If you have pierced this part of your body then you haven't even thought of its potential to be nurturing. You have identified the breast as being strictly sexual."

Of course body piercing and tattooing are not specific to females, as males are showing up at tattoo parlors in droves in order to express in permanent ink the anger and emotional turbulence that lies beneath their skin. Ms. Anderson-Decelles believes that the younger males enter the program earlier because they act out, and that this may be the way they are getting their needs met. They often steal as a way to survive, fight because it is the only way that they can maintain some sense of self-esteem even though the quick-fix will last only a short time before the cycle of self-loathing sets in. They are angry and confused as to why they are not getting their needs met, and acting out is a frustrated attempt to get people to notice, which for the most part, works. Of course, getting noticed for their negative behavior reinforces these kids to act out, but Ms. Anderson-Decelles says that, "I would rather have an angry, raging kid any day than one who is withdrawn. It as if they are aware on some level that they deserve to be loved and paid attention to and they are expressing this outrage of being wronged by their parents in a very loud voice." This is especially true of the males who have been abused. They have a deep-seeded anger towards their mothers for not protecting them. Whether their mothers were aware of the abuse or not, does not seem to matter, as kids have an inherent sense of a mother's omnipotent ability to protect and shield her cubs from the world and its dangers. Especially boys, as the opposite gender dynamic is present, feel an overwhelming sense of love and devotion towards their mothers at the same time. These contradictory emotions reap havoc within these young males. On some level they know these feelings are valid, yet they feel guilty for feeling this way towards their own mothers and begin to hate themselves for it.

Ms. Anderson-Decelles explains that over half of the children in the program come from an impoverished home environment. These are kids who have never been to the beach, a movie theatre, or a restaurant other than McDonald's. When they were younger, they may have had a television, but they lacked books and toys that had any value as far as enhancing creative or intellectual development. These are children who have suffered nutritionally as well. For the most part, they have been on diets high in fat, sugar, and caffeine from the beginning, which has affected their growth as well as their behavior. This is not to say that parents who have not had the same opportunities as others are destined to be bad parents. On the contrary, I have seen more parents than I would like to admit who would be considered middle class, upper-middle class, and in some cases wealthy, who did not have two parenting skills to rub together. I have had parents walk in and open their checkbooks with the intention of merely wanting me to *fix* their child.

When Ms. Anderson-Decelles speaks of attachment theory, she explains that, "it has never been a theory of rocket science. Attachment theory has always been about what Winnicott and Ainsworth universally describe as the *"good enough parent.* It has never been about significant education. It has never been about significant economic achievement. It has never been about significant intellectual ability. The success of a child rests on the good enough parent, and that means a parent, who is consistently, from the beginning, child focused." Ms. Anderson-Decelles goes on to say that in no way does a good enough parent insinuate "a *perfect* parent. It doesn't mean a parent who gets tired or cranky and doesn't want to just ship that kid off to somebody else. It doesn't mean a parent who has four kids, and when they are on the third day of the flu for the third kid, feels like they just can't get out of bed one more time to rub their child's back and keep their hair out of their face while they throw up. Attachment means consistently being there from the beginning and seeing things through for the long haul. The very success of early attachment rests on an infant, from the beginning, feeling nurtured, comforted, and sated. They need to be held and they need to feel satisfied."

Ms. Anderson-Decelles continues to describe attachment as getting "more complicated as kids naturally become more independent. There are, for example, parents who are fabulous with babies and then have a really difficult time with toddler-hood. Toddler-hood is where children begin to become autonomous and necessarily so, however, they lack both the physiological and cognitive capacity to really be independent." This is where consistency with limit-setting comes into play. It is when a toddler veers off the playground to explore, attempts to ride a tricycle without a helmet, or resolves a sand box conflict by hitting or pushing, that the parent needs to impose limits. These limits serve as *walls* for the child to bounce off of in order to figure out which is the best way to go. They help the child to navigate his or her behavior. Ms. Anderson-Decelles goes on to discuss that, "parenting gets progressively more difficult, and the *good enough* parent learns as he or she goes along."

It is quite clear at this point that satisfying basic needs is not enough, as even experiments done with Rhesus monkeys have proven. When the monkeys were given enough to eat and adequate shelter, but were kept from being held or comforted, they died. Ms. Anderson-Decelles explains that, "the kids who are in the worst dilemma, are the kids who have had what I call sporadic nurturing, or nurturing that is unreliable. Nurturing that is parent-oriented rather than child-oriented that says, 'I am going to meet your needs when it is convenient for me, when it looks good for me, when I want to, when you are pleasing me, or when I feel like I care about you.' To me, this is the most damaging form of attachment or nurturance."

All children have an inherent need to be loved and nurtured unconditionally, without ties to external circumstances, feelings, or behavior. When a child's needs are met only sporadically, Ms. Anderson-Decelles explains that, "they have to try to begin to understand what is going on. Kids seek order to their world. They seek to understand their environment, therefore the kid who is sporadically nurtured starts questioning what is wrong with him." She will begin to wonder what it is she is or is not doing that is causing her not to get her needs met. She will question what is wrong with her. Ms. Anderson-Decelles says that when a parent nurtures sporadically that the child, "will begin to internalize a sense of inherent flaw. They begin to believe that there is something wrong with them. They begin to believe that when Mom is treating them well it is because they have done something right. When Mom is not treating them well and not meeting their needs it is because they have somehow not met her expectations, or there is something broken, burdened, or wrong about them." The problem with this, she says, "is that these feelings are constantly reinforced because the sporadic nurturer *repeatedly* fails to meet needs. The child begins to feel even more flawed than they did to begin with. The child then begins to feel ashamed, unloved, insecure, and anxious."

Of course, naturally, the child will begin to figure out what it is that he or she needs to do or say to receive attention from their primary parent. A select few, with the innate ability and emotional maturity to be self-motivated and to rely on internal self-approval will still thrive. These *survivors*, however, are the exception and not the rule. For most of these children who have not had their needs met, or who have been given affection and attention only when their parent has been in the mood to do so, will begin to seek out attention any way they can get it. And, as for the most part, since positive attention primarily goes unnoticed by the sporadic nurturer, the child will be begin to act out. This is the age old dynamic of negative attention is better than no attention at all.

The problem with this hit or miss attention Ms. Anderson-Decelles explains, "is that these kids learn to separate feeling from action. They begin to believe that their actions are not necessarily related to their feelings. At the same time, when they are separating their feelings from their actions, there are also moments when the sporadically nurtured child sees feelings and actions as one in the same." These kids, for the most part, are unable to label their feelings accurately, internally or verbally. They have not yet made the connection that the sadness they may be feeling stemmed from the feeling of loneliness from being left out of a group or activity. The sadness may then lead to frustration because nothing they are doing to be a part of things seems to be working. The frustration then leads to anger. The anger turns into a fistfight which results in being seated in the principal's office with recess privileges being taken away for a week. They are unable to see this connection, and Ms. Anderson-Decelles explains "that if you were to pull a sporadically nurtured adolescent out of a fist fight and asked him what caused it, that he would respond with a blanket statement such as 'I was really pissed off'. The connection of his feelings with his actions would be missing completely."

As the primary parent, for whatever reason, was unable to take the time to be emotionally present on a consistent basis when these children were younger, these kids need to be taught to process their feelings. They need to be taught to understand the connection between feelings and actions by being walked through the sequence of events that lead up to the inappropriate or undesirable behavior. Just like anything else, they need to learn to do so with repetition and consistency, in order put in place, as much as is possible at this point in their development, what was missing during their early, formative, years. Ms. Anderson-Decelles further explains that if you took the time to walk the preteen or teen all the way back to the source of his anger, that he would respond with something such as, "people don't like me very much." It is in these situations, she says, "that the teen's *feeling space* becomes very small and his *action space* becomes very big, whereas in a healthy, attached kid, this is the opposite. The attached kid has a large *feeling space* and an *action space* that becomes smaller."

Ms. Anderson-Decelles goes on to say that, "kids who do not react physically or hurt anybody have feelings just as powerful. They get just as sad, angry, and frustrated, however, they have learned to *feel* those feelings, and then to *think* about what those feelings mean. In the healthy, attached child, the cognitive piece mitigates the emotional piece the majority of the time. They can then, from a whole plethora of choices, stay inside themselves and access their own internal resources. They can realize that they are feeling sad, lonely, or frustrated, and still feel o.k. with themselves because they have an inherent sense of being loved. They can experience negative feelings and yet simultaneously access the awareness that they are still a good kid." In no way does this mean that an attached kid cannot lose it and punch somebody in the nose, however, *most of the time* there is a solid, cognitive connection between feelings and actions. There is also more of an awareness of consequences, and an ability to *weigh out* whether or not it is worth it to react in a certain situation. The healthy, attached kid can experience negative emotion without internalizing that negativity as a feeling of inherent worthlessness.

What is difficult for psychologists and therapists working with children who have been sporadically nurtured, Ms. Anderson-Decelles explains, is that "we are always working from the outside in, and it can be really challenging. Integration, of course, means from the inside out. When you are working with kids who have been sporadically nurtured, however, and who have anxious attachments, avoidant attachments, or no attachments, you are working from the outside in. Much of this difficulty has to do with the fact that these teens are so incapable of identifying and accurately labeling their feelings. They are so particularly defended against such feelings as sadness, loneliness, alienation, and fear. This is because these feelings are the most primal of the emotional spectrum, and therefore, these are the feelings that will build up the most pervasive and powerful defense mechanisms. We find ourselves working through layers and layers of coping strategies." A healthy, attached teen, when you eventually access the source of his or her loneliness, will seek reassurance and emotional validation. A sporadically nurtured teen, on the other hand, Ms. Anderson-Decelles explains, "will seek alleviation of feeling. They are looking to be emotionally anesthetized. They do not want to feel."

There is an obvious correlation between teens not wanting to feel and *self-medicating* with drugs and alcohol. These kids are more at ease when they are numb and feeling no pain. Of course once the affects of whatever it is they are taking wear off, they wake up to the same problems in addition to any related messes they created for themselves while being under the influence. Kids with attachment issues who have developed anxiety will often self-medicate this way also as a way for them to regulate their nervous energy and fears. These same kids whose anxiety has manifested as depression, may also attempt to turn to drugs and alcohol as a way to cope. They soon find out that the depressive affects of alcohol on the brain further exacerbate their feelings of sadness, and send them deeper into their dark and lonely world. These are frequently the kids who take their lives. They may have had fleeting thoughts of suicide, wondering if it would be a better deal than what they have now, then with a little extra push from alcohol to give them the guts they need, take their final action to permanently end their pain.

As discussed previously, there is a certain percentage of preteens and teens who would be considered to be struggling with an organically based mental illness, however, for the majority of medicated kids out there, I strongly believe this is not the case. We have never before had so many children, preteens, and teens diagnosed with major mental illnesses, and I do not accept that this outrageously high number of *sick* kids has always existed and that we are just now beginning to *realize and label these illnesses and disorders.* We seem to be far too concerned with what is politically correct and on not passing judgement, when the reality is that when we become parents we take on the biggest, most important job in the world. We accept the responsibility for another life. Of course, most of us are doing the best we can with our children, emotionally, spiritually, financially, educationally, and with our relationship situations. We are working hard at being *good enough* parents, not perfect, but simply *good enough.*

As most of us are also aware, parenting is a job full of rewards, but it is also hard work that takes dedication and emotional stamina. Unfortunately, if the effort and energy are not there even for reasons that may seem overwhelming or unavoidable, the child is still directly affected. Just as a seedling cannot thrive without water, nutrients, and the warmth of the sun, so it is true with our children. Without *our* warmth and care they cannot grow. Without our attention and effort to pull out the intrusive weeds around them they cannot grow. This, in my opinion, is nothing short of tragic, as our children, teens, and young adults are invaluable treasure and our future. It is the area where we devote the majority our time, attention, and energy, that will be successful, whether it be our careers, making money, our bodies, our golf game, or our relationships. It is our actions that matter to our kids. We can *say* anything we want to, but what they *hear* when we are doing anything else but spending time with them, is that they are last on our list. They are not important. Showing up at soccer games, having dinner together, knowing who their friends are and caring about what they are up to, all translates into "I love you and you are important to me."

Of course, much has been written lately on the rising numbers of teen depression, suicides, anxiety disorders, conduct disorders, oppositional defiant disorders, and budding personality disorders, and, in particular, kids with bipolar disorder. This is the current term used to describe extreme mood fluctuation, and is synonymous with what used to be labeled manic-depression. The child or adult who suffers from bipolar disorder experiences periods of low moods followed by a surge of impulsive energy where he or she is almost in a euphoric state of mind, often unaware of and unable to control their actions. Though there is much evidence relating bipolar disorder to genes and heredity, there is also some attention being paid to the potential for a child to be predisposed to the disorder and the relationship to his or her environmental circumstances. According to *Time's* Jeffrey Kluger and Sora Song, who write in their article *Young and Bipolar* that, "Determining why the age-of-onset figures are in free fall is attracting a lot of research attention. Some experts believe that kids are being tipped into bipolar disorder by family and school stress, recreational drug use and perhaps even a collection of genes that express themselves more aggressively in each generation." They continue to say that, "bipolar disorder is not an illness that can be allowed to go untreated. Victims have an alcoholism and drug-abuse rate triple that of the rest of the population and a suicide rate that may approach 20%." Just as with any other mental illness, it is also possible that it has masked itself as something else and been misdiagnosed as attention deficit disorder, conduct disorder, or oppositional defiant disorder as the symptoms are similar, or it may have gone completely unnoticed.

Bipolar Disorder has become the sort of the diagnosis du jour, much like Attention Deficit Disorder was a decade ago. A certain number of kids really and truly struggle with a physiological and neurological condition, while others are the products of their environments. The same is true for anxiety. Some kids are genetically set up to have a tough road, while others have had no rules, no limits, and no consistency, and have therefore had no walls to bounce off of in order to figure out who they are or the parameters of their world. Because of this they do not have any internal sense of security. I couldn't possibly guess at the numbers of kids that have been referred to me for anxiety problems. In many cases, once we were able to work with the family as a unit, to get some supports in place as far as parenting skills and education, and to establish some firm limits and behavioral guidelines, things improved dramatically. In some cases, the anxiety completely dissipated.

It is important to discuss the issue of misdiagnosis as it happens so frequently, especially with children. I have worked with children and their families for quite a long time and I have seen a broad spectrum of emotional and behavioral difficulties, as well as a variety of very interesting family dynamics. Usually the child would be the initial referral following a series of behavioral episodes. Many times the child would be misdiagnosed. In fact, I would automatically raise an eyebrow if the child came in with a diagnosis of ADD. More often than not, the child would be medicated for the convenience of his teachers and parents. They had *had it* with little so and so's acting out and decided that she must have ADHD, which is an easy blanket diagnosis to throw over a child who chooses not to conform or passively go along with the adult world when things are not right in her world. This is also an easy diagnosis to get for your child if you want to since it is based on very subjective information from teachers and family members. If a parent wants to see it she will and if she looks hard enough she can find a psychologist, or pediatrician for that matter, who will prescribe Ritalin or some other drug. Of course, as the family became more a part of the child's treatment plan, things would inevitably begin to unfold. Not always, but frequently, the problem lied in the parenting department. They were usually inconsistent with limits, non-attentive, or overindulgent. There was usually a lack of time, attention, or general interest in their child's world. There was little positive interaction. These parents didn't know who their child's best friend was at school or what part of the day they looked forward to the most.

Again, there is no doubt that some children are unfortunately *dealt a bad hand* as they say, not different than a child being born with Type I Diabetes who will need to take shots of insulin for the rest of his or her life. No one did anything to cause it. It just is what it is and they will need to learn to manage it on a daily basis if they want a live a healthy, high quality life. This is not different with some people who struggle with depression, anxiety, bipolar disorder, and other mood disorders and mental illnesses. It is also possible that the potential for a mood disorder or mental illness may be there, but with a *good enough parent*, and a stable home environment, remains dormant. As parents, we have tremendous power and influence over our children's lives and well being, and unfortunately, we have the capability to bring forth or trigger these symptoms in a child by abuse, neglect, or the cumulative affect of inconsistent nurturing.

PART V

Parents and the *Road Less Traveled*

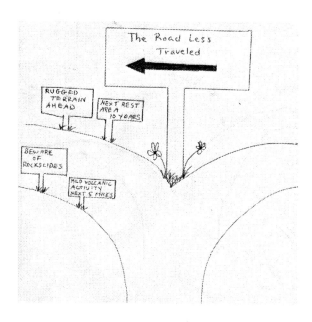

18

Single Dads

*It is hardly possible to begin to describe the ways in which
a father enriches the life of his children, so wide are the possibilities.*

—*D.W. Winnicott*

Being the parent of a teenager is enough to warrant the world's sympathy, but to take on this challenge alone presents an even higher mountain to climb with far more rockslides and avalanches. Not to say that being a single parent of a child of any age isn't challenge enough, as these parents are both mother and father, breadwinner and homemaker, but to guide a child through the turbulence of adolescence alone adds a different dimension to single parenthood. This is especially true if the single parent is a dad as the vast majority of our nation's single parents are moms. As unfortunate as it is, society is used to women going it alone as men are *usually* the ones to leave and moms are *usually* the ones left behind to figure it all out and make it work. This truthful generalization is also something that is changing. More and more women are walking out, leaving Dad behind and the kids to visit her every other weekend.

I spoke with several single dads who have *full* custody of their children, specifically preteens and teenagers, to hear what their perspectives were on raising these kids completely by themselves and how they feel as far as being accepted and supported by their communities. One single dad of a thirteen year old boy talked about the pressures of being the primary parent and said, "now it is my job alone to make sure that my son has a bed time and that his homework is done, that he does his chores around the house, and that there are consequences for his actions." He continued to say how frustrating it is sometimes that, "the *weekend parent* gets to be the *fun parent* and does not have to share the daily burden of parental responsibility as far as setting limits and being consistent with household rules. She also does not have to arrange or attend dentist appointments, sports physicals, or stay awake when her child is throwing up with the flu." He said that "it is like my son has the Disneyland experience and then he comes home. This obviously creates problems on the home front as my son has to readjust to having rules and going to bed at a certain time in order to wake up for school the next day. There is no more eating ice cream bars on the couch late at night or unlimited television watching. It is something we struggle with every time he goes to see his mother. In fact, I feel that I am set up to be the bad guy when what it really is, is that I am the parent he lives with day in and day out so I am the one that has to be the limit setter and rule enforcer. When he goes to his mother's house once or twice a month to stay over night, he is essentially on vacation."

As far as life at home, Single Dad says that his son spends a lot of time waiting. Single Dad says that it has been this way since Mom left when his son was six years old. He was then working with a small construction company and had to bring his son along on jobs as the school's kindergarten was only half day and daycare was more than he could afford at the time. He also did not have any family members living less than four hours away. The time spent waiting would increase once school let out and working hours increased as summer was peak season for construction work. Single Dad said that his son would just have to sit off to the side out of the danger zone with a couple of toys until his work day was over.

Now that his son is thirteen he is still going along with his Dad to work. Single Dad is now a custodian for the public school in his town and gets up at 5:00 am each day. He is also sometimes there late at night when there are sports events. Single Dad says that, "my son is old enough to be left alone for a short time, and I will leave him briefly to run to the store, but I do not want him to come home to an empty house after school or to have to leave an empty house to start his day, especially because he is the only child. It could get lonely." Single Dad is fortunate to have flexible hours working for the school system. He works while his son is in school and then when his son has soccer games, he manipulates his schedule so that he can be there for every game. This is also true for Single Dad when his son gets sick. As there is no net, he has to stay home with his sick child and then make up the hours when he comes back to work.

When asked about what is most challenging about being the primary parent, Single Dad said that he finds it difficult to "not have anyone right there to bounce ideas off of." He says that, "every parent has moments where they question whether they are handling a certain situation in the best way or whether they said the right thing, and it is hard to rely only on yourself. It would be so much easier to have someone to share the decision-making with. All you can do is the best that you can." Single Dad says also that though he considers himself to be nurturing that he feels badly that his son is not getting the same kind of nurturing that a mother can provide. Single Dad says that, "I think that men are just wired differently. We are more task oriented and more apt to try and fix a situation. Like when a child gets hurt a mother would give him all kinds of attention and kind of goop and gush all over him. I just want to put a bandaid on tell him to get over it. Let's move on here." Also without having a mom living with them, Single Dad worries about relationship modeling and that his son will have no idea how to treat a woman or what a healthy relationship looks like.

Single Dad also says that he finds it challenging to not have much time for himself. He works all day and through the evening if there is a sports event, then has dinner to make, and homework to supervise. Mom takes his son overnight a couple of times a month often without much notice, which can make it difficult to make plans. Single Dad says that one thing that he does in his free time is play golf and he brings his son with him. According to Single Dad, his son "is learning to be a really good golfer." They also have a weekly ritual of getting Chinese take out on Friday nights that they both look forward to. As far as support, Single Dad does feel that he is accepted within his community and that overall people are very supportive. Single Dad said that his family all live out of state, but that he has developed a solid network of friends that are there for him if he needs them.

Another single dad tells his story that has the added element of a male parent raising children of the opposite gender. All three of his girls are close in age, the oldest being thirteen and in junior high school. This single dad tells me that he got full custody of the girls approximately six years ago following a phone call he received at work. The person on the other end told him that he needed to come and pick up the girls from school, as their mother had overdosed on drugs and was being rushed to the hospital. Mom apparently gave up the kids voluntarily following the overdose as she considered herself to be mentally unfit, as well as the fact that she was unable to provide a suitable living environment. Single Dad told me, "that the girls' mother saw them anywhere from once a week, to once a month, to once every three months. The visits were very sporadic and sometimes required some persuasion."

As far as child support payments, the original agreement involved Mom paying little child support if she would agree to take the kids when needed. Mom paid Single Dad for only the first few months and he says, "that if I added up all of the back child support she owes, that it would be somewhere in the vicinity of 14,000 dollars and this is at the rate of a mere 178 dollars a month. When she had custody of the kids, I was paying almost a thousand dollars a month, and it came straight out of my paycheck." Single Dad continues to say, "that I haven't gone after her for the back child support. I just want her to have a relationship with the girls. I don't care if she has a daughter, but I do care that the girls have a mother. They need to have a mother."

As far as his work schedule, Single Dad tells me that he is a correctional officer in a nearby prison facility. The security level of the facility is medium-maximum and is the largest prison in the state. He wakes up at 4:30 am to be at work by 6:00 am, as he has an hour commute. When he arrives, he deals with murderers and sex offenders, though he tells me that the majority of the inmates are there for drug related offenses. He continues to tell me about his own observations as far as the downtown area where he lives, and comments that he has noticed that the number of young kids on the street has risen dramatically. Single Dad says that whether we can help it or not, that "society has dictated how things are going to be as far as families needing two incomes to survive, and that with both parents working that there is no one home to watch the kids. It seems like there is less and less time being spent with kids. This has steam-rolled into kids being out on the street. When I was young, you never saw eight and ten year old kids out on the street, and now they are everywhere. I believe that someone has got to be home full time to have a positive influence on the kids. It has gone from one generation to another, and it seems to me that our family values have really dropped."

Single Dad continues to discuss what he sees on his shift as a senior correctional officer. He says, "These kids, meaning the eighteen to twenty-two year olds, just don't care. They have this attitude. The attitude is What are you going to do to me, and the reality is that the consequences of their behavior is very much in our hands. They just don't care. They have never had stable lives. They have never had anyone to say no to them. It seems that they do not have respect for anyone or anything, and it seems that it is trickling down from one generation to another. Believe it or not, there was a time when we had a father and his three sons in the same prison at the same time. It's disturbing." Single Dad commented that he feels that our family values have really plummeted and that he is concerned about the direction our society is headed in. As far as his own family, he is thankful for having such a large, close knit family, as they have been able to fill in the gaps and be there for the girls when he has needed them to be.

As far as the challenges of a being a single father, this dad talked about one of the toughest moments being when his older daughter began to menstruate for the first time last year. Single Dad said, "She was pretty afraid to talk about it with me, but I noticed the day that it happened. I noticed that she was having stomach cramps, then I went in and noticed that there was stuff in the toilet. Fortunately, we have a lot of family nearby. I called my sister right away and she came right over to talk with her. She pretty much had the mother-daughter talk with her." Another issue as far as raising children of the opposite gender is the bath routine at night. Single Dad says, "It is difficult to make sure that your kids have a decent bath. When you are a man and they are little girls, you can't actually go in and wash their hair for them. It is difficult. They have their grandmother sometimes, and my sister. In fact, when the girls were younger, my sister had to come over every morning to help me get them ready for school just for this reason." Of course, no one would raise an eyebrow to a single mother giving her son a bath, but a father bathing a little girl has the obvious sexual taboo attached to it.

Single Dad says that his biggest challenge is juggling his schedule. He works the 6:00 am until 2:00pm shift, then after his hour long commute gets home just a few minutes before the school bus arrives. He tells me that the biggest stress for him is having to race back home in order to be there for the bus. When he gets home he has to check homework, do laundry, and make dinner. Single Dad says that he has learned to enjoy cooking and is now grateful that he took home economics in junior high and high school. They try to sit down for dinner as much as possible, but Single Dad says that, "one of toughest things about managing a schedule is the sports and after school activities. After working eight hours, and driving, it is hard sometimes. My family has helped me out in this way also. I don't know what I would do without them."

For the most part, Single Dad says that his supervisors and co-workers have been supportive. When he first got the call about his ex-wife's overdose, he was granted two weeks of family leave time. They also have something called mandatory over-time where the correctional facility needs to have someone fill a slot in the following shift. It is volunteer at first, then if no one steps forward, someone is chosen from a rotating list. Single Dad says that the supervisors on occasion have gone against facility rules and ordered someone else because he was unable to find someone to watch his girls on such short notice. He says, "I have also made a good faith effort when it has been my turn to find someone to take the girls if at all possible. I would stay if I was able to work it out." Single Dad continues, "the challenging thing about these days is the additional four hours added to my work day. I have to make up the time on the other end. When I get home four hours later, I still have the laundry, dinner, dishes, and homework waiting for me. I would have everything else to make up for, my other job."

Single Dad and I then talked about how juggling all of these balls in the air is something that single mothers have been doing for years, and how the numbers of men now doing the same thing is beginning to grow. The obvious deduction is that trying to manage two full-time jobs is a quite a challenge for anyone. To be able to pull it off without losing your mind or having a heart attack, support systems must be in place and an effort made to take care of the care-giver whenever possible.

Just as there is a *Super Mom Syndrome*, so it is true with dads. Chuck Gregg, Ph.D. writes in *Single Fatherhood* that, "the Super Dad Syndrome has to do with single fathers believing they can be all things at all times for their children without the need for any time off or outside help." One of the main reasons that single fathers try to be everybody's everything has a large part to do with the guilt they feel. Gregg says that, "Single fathers may harbor feelings of guilt over not being able to make their marriages work. Since the children have already experienced the trauma of divorce, single fathers try to shield them from any further psychological harm by doing everything for them." He continues to explain that, Single fathers may fear they will be rejected by their children, especially if they make demands on their time or ask for their cooperation in maintaining the household. It some cases this fear may be well founded particularly in cases of custody disputes where both parents feel compelled to fight for their children's love and approval."

Not different from most of us moms, Gregg says that, "Some single fathers actually believe they can be all things at all times for their children. In other words, they buy into the notion that they can be Super Dads. They choose to ignore the more obvious signs of stress in their lives. They fail to appreciate the hole they are ultimately digging for themselves." Just like men are not known for their ability to stop and ask for directions when they are lost, Gregg says that, "Some single fathers fail to appreciate the reality of things. They get themselves into deeper and deeper trouble, yet they stubbornly refuse to accept any outside help. When asked, they say they are working things out fine on their own."

Finally, Gregg discusses Single Dads and their relationship to perfectionism, which in our home is referred to as the "P word." In fact, due to the highly abusive nature of this condition or state of mind, my children are not allowed to use the word in the house. My oldest son came up with *99 percent excellent* as a substitute, which my five children have now adopted as part of their daily vocabulary. Certainly, moms are more than familiar with the "P word" and what it does to us to constantly compare ourselves with those around us as well as all of the should's and ought to's which exist only in our minds. These mental rehearsals can and often do go on all day long, where we measure ourselves, and therefore our self worth, against others real or imagined. The result of these daily internal dialogues is perpetually feeling inadequate, as if we are not doing enough, and basically feeling overall lousy about ourselves. Gregg states that, "Being a single father means being able to accept the fact that the world is going to be less than perfect. It may mean not having a clean shirt to wear, not coming home to a hot dinner at night, not having the house kept neat as a pin. Men who strive to maintain a perfect lifestyle when they become single fathers are bound to run into problems."

Gregg talks about what signs to look for if you think that you are suffering from the Super Dad Syndrome (which are basically the same for the Super Mom Syndrome). First of all, fathers need to pay attention to their energy levels. Gregg says that single fathers are often "easily fatigued. You are completely bushed at the end of the day. It is all you can do to stay awake through the evening to watch a favorite television show. Even routine chores around the house leave you exhausted. You spend your weekends resting up but it does not seem to do any good. In addition, your resistance to disease is not what it used to be. You seem to catch every cold or flu bug going around. You find yourself using up more sick days at work." Gregg continues to say that may single fathers experience sleep disturbance. This can mean either too much or too little. He says that, "You are sleeping much more than usual...But the additional sleep does not seem to make much of a difference. Or, he says, "You are exhausted when you go to bed...Yet halfway through the night you are suddenly awake. Your mind is spinning with all the things that need doing and all the projects left unfinished." Changes in eating habits may also occur.

Most importantly, Gregg says, "The more you try to be Super Dad, the more is expected from you. Rather than simplifying your life you are actually making it more complicated. Rather than solving problems, you are creating new ones. It is as if you are caught in a giant whirlpool. You are gradually being sucked lower and lower and you feel unable to do anything about it." Usually following feelings of chronic fatigue, anxiety, frustration, and an overall feeling of being overwhelmed, comes the feeling of hopelessness. These feelings discussed as being the criteria of the Super Dad Syndrome are also many of the symptoms of depression. There is usually a general feeling that one's efforts do not matter so why bother trying. Since depression and anxiety go together, underneath these feelings of hopelessness is usually a nervous feeling. People who are depressed or "stuck in a rut" as some might say, are edgy and often snap over nothing. Finally, many people will get down on themselves when they have felt this way for an extended period of time. They may feel that they deserve to feel this way.

This is a good time to get some help and support, even though it is the last thing that a depressed single parent may want to do. Therapy is always a good idea. There are also many parenting support groups out there comprised of people who have been down the same road. Most people who have asked for help through support groups will speak positively of the experience, whether they are single parents, alcoholics, or people who have just lost a loved one and are in need of bereavement support. There is strength in sharing life experiences and allowing oneself to be vulnerable in a trusted situation. Not only this, but often friendships develop because people have so much in common. Of course if these feelings of hopelessness and helplessness do not dissipate, then professional treatment should be sought.

19

Same-sex Parenting

"*For most straight people, becoming a parent is like going to school. Every-body does it, but without really thinking about it. Yet parenting is one of the most important functions in life, something for which people should be emo-*

tionally, mentally, and psychologically prepared, something that takes a lot of work, doesn't happen overnight, and deserves some prior soul-searching."

—Dr. Stephanie Schacher
—clinical psychologist

—from *Gay Dads* by David Strah

When first deciding to get going on a second book, after writing *Striving for the Purple Heart* which is primarily geared towards young motherhood, I visualized a book that addressed issues and concerns for *all* parents of *all* teens, not simply *straight* parents of *straight* teens. At present, gay people make up approximately 10 percent of the population, and as our society gradually becomes more tolerant of alternate life-styles, more and more adults as well as teens are *coming out* and therefore able to live full and happy lives. It is also becoming a possibility for same-sex couples to have the American dream of a family and a home in a neighborhood, complete with a white picket fence and a Subaru parked in the driveway. Same-sex couples now have the options of adoption, choosing a surrogate parent, or artificial insemination, in order to begin a family life. Some Family Health Centers are now offering parenting education courses, counseling, and support groups for same-sex parents.

Same-sex couples have been adopting children for years, yet the very controversial issue of same-sex marriage continues to be an on-going source of heated debate. Even in the case of civil union, which is simply a *legally* binding contract that protects the rights of both partners, yet without any affiliation with religion, appears to cause agita among the conservatives as well. All this commitment is about, from a legal standpoint, is protecting both partners in the event of chronic illness or death as far as custody of their children and their possessions. It seems to me that if two people have been together for thirty years, and one of them dies, that the good silver shouldn't end up with Aunt Matilda. By preventing these very basic civil rights many of the children of same-sex couples are also affected. They lack the security of knowing, that if something happened to one parent that they would automatically still have their other parent. April Martin. Ph.D. writes in her article *Same-sex Marriage & Parenting* that, "Same-sex couples are not biological procreative units, but they are nevertheless parents. They raise children in families where, most often, one parent is related only by devotion and hard work to the biological children of the other. The children rely on them, often calling both women "Mom," or both men "Dad." But because they can't get married, non-biological parents feel the ever present danger that a court may not even view them as relevant parties in a custody decision if the biological parent should die or the relationship end in separation. And their children live with the ongoing insecurity that losing one parent in a tragedy might simultaneously mean losing the other parent in a courtroom."

I was able to interview several couples from across the country to hear what their experiences as same-sex parents and grandparents have been like for them, as well as to hear what some of their concerns were and continue to be. The first couple I interviewed, were two women from the Los Angeles area of California who had been together for about a year when they decided to have children. Both partners had been working in the childcare field for quite a few years, which is where they first met. In addition to working as childcare providers for a corporate daycare, one of the partners also currently teaches gymnastics to preschool children.

Once they decided to have children, California Mom-to-be went on the Internet to find out how to begin the artificial insemination process. She found a sperm bank called the Cryo Bank, and began to research an appropriate fit for she and her partner as they wanted to have their baby closely resemble their own genetic make-up, as well as each partner's heritage and decent. California Mom-to-be's partner then informed me of how involved this initial step was. The sperm donor is not only screened for any undesirable or threatening medical history, but his family is as well. California Partner informed me that the sperm bank screened information regarding the donor's grandparents, aunts, uncles, and siblings. They screened for anything that was potentially dangerous medically in each extended family member, as well as what their educational levels were, their career history, lifestyles, goals and desires. The couple was also given a childhood photo of the donor, as well as a sketch of what he may look like currently, and an audio. California Partner said that she had no idea that this part of the process would be "so extensive," and that the irony here is that in the heterosexual world, "it can take so much longer to find out such detailed information about your partner's family history."

California Mom-to-be said that from selection to insemination, the process took approximately three months and the cost about two thousand dollars. It is suggested that a couple purchase six vials of sperm as the process of insemination is normally done over several consecutive days in order to increase the chances of the egg being fertilized. Once they purchased the sperm, the couple made an appointment with a licensed practitioner who preformed the artificial insemination. The first insemination *took*, leaving the couple with two vials of sperm which are being stored in the event they want to have more children in the future. The couple was thrilled to find out they were going to have a baby, and now are thrilled to find out that they are having a little girl.

When I asked them about any concerns they may have as far as raising a child in a same-sex household, California Mom-to-be aid, "I worry about how she will be treated by other people because of our life-style. I have also done some reading, and one of the most common problems for children of same-sex couples is that they can sometimes feel ashamed and embarrassed. I have read that they sometimes want to hide their family life. One thing I am not worried about is that I know that we will be great parents." California Partner feels the same way, and further elaborates on how much the couple wants this child. She says, "that in the heterosexual world it doesn't take much for someone to knock somebody else up, with no thought put into the consequences." California Mom-to-be then explains, "that since for a gay or lesbian couple this cannot happen by accident, lots of thought and preparation goes into having a child together. We really *want* her. In fact, we are not due until March, and already her room is painted with the border up. Her bed is made, and she has a full wardrobe in the closet. We even have diapers in the drawer. We have the stroller and the car seat. We don't have wipes yet, but we are going to Costco next week and we'll get some then."

Some of their other concerns they tell me, "aren't different than any other parents. We are concerned about school systems, and the community she will live in. This is why we have decided to move before she enters school to southern Pasadena, where the school system is better, and people are far more accepting. Right now, we technically fall in the Los Angeles district and there is no way we want to bring our daughter up here. If not Pasadena, then maybe Vermont. I have also heard really good things about New Paltz, New York. It is apparently a really progressive town, open to alternative lifestyles." California Partner then added, "We need to find a community that is open-minded and accepting because of our lifestyle, but also because ethnically, we are a racially diverse family. Our daughter will have this to contend with also, so it is important that we find the right community." California Mom-to-be then summed up with, "At least she won't have worries as far as her family and home life, as we have a very solid relationship. We have our differences just as any couple does, but we solve them in a respectful manner. We communicate really well."

California Partner then added, "As far as the getting excited part goes, I think that I may know what it is like to feel like a husband whose wife is having a baby, because my partner is the one going through the physical part. I think about how the baby will bond with me." The couple has, however, taken care of things as far as custody should something happen to either partner. They had a commitment ceremony this year and have filed for their *Declaration of Domestic Partnership* with the state of California. The rules for this legally recognized commitment are that both partners are over eighteen years of age, are not married or in another domestic partnership, are living together, are the same sex or one of the partners is over the age of 62. Once the domestic partnership is granted by the state of California, both partners have the legal rights that a marriage would guarantee, primarily the making of medical decisions, becoming the primary beneficiaries of mutual finances, as well as the custody of any children had together. According to this couple, this is new and became affective January 1st, 2005. What is also new, is that the partner who is not the biological parent of a child conceived through artificial insemination, is no longer required to formally adopt her own child. Prior to January 1st, 2005, this was the case.

The other type of same-sex parent, is the person who either didn't realize their sexual orientation until after they were married with children, or they did know who they are and were not yet *able* to come out. They may not have found the strength or the courage until after they were married to face the consequences of revealing who they are (and have always been) to their close friends and family members. Such is the case with one gay dad from Texas who has been with his partner for fourteen years.

When I asked Texas Dad how old he was when he realized that he was different from other boys, he responded with, "at about four years old." Texas Dad had grown up in a Hispanic family where boys were expected to do rough things and be "macho." Ironically, Texas Dad's uncle was outwardly gay and with his partner for almost 50 years before his partner died. The family reportedly accepted the uncle, but later would have a difficult time when Texas Dad announced the same news.

At twenty years old, Texas Dad joined the military. As if that was not enough, he joined the Mormon Church also, and said that when he confided in some new friends at the Church that their response was that he should just find the right girl and he'd be just fine. Shortly thereafter, Texas Dad was married and said that after the first night with her, "I knew that this was not what I wanted. It was depressing trying to not be who I was." They were married for fifteen years, and it was towards the end of the fourteenth year that Texas Dad said "he just couldn't take it anymore" and he decided to tell his wife about his desires. As Texas Dad loved his children and the family life, he tried to persuade her to let him talk about his desires when he needed to and that maybe the family could stay in tact. His ex-wife responded with, "I don't want you to talk about it or think about it. When we have sex, I want you to think of me and not being with a man." Texas

Dad explained that he could no longer do that. The couple tried to see a counselor and things "went down hill very quickly. I tried very hard to keep the marriage, but everything was against it. She wanted me out of the house. I had to get an apartment. I had no furniture and no money. We went to a judge in Texas and my ex-wife got it all, the kids and the house. I got nothing. It was all because I was gay."

Texas Dad said that he became very depressed and contemplated suicide. He said, "that it was so difficult to say good-bye to the children who were then eight, ten, twelve, and fourteen. I had to call my dad and tell him that I had lost my apartment and that I didn't have any more money. He came all the way out to California where I had moved and was surprised to see how I had been living." During this whole time, Texas Dad said, "I would call my children every week, send them letters, and arrange visits through the court like I was supposed to. I could hear my children in the background while my ex-wife told me that they were not in the house. All of the letters I sent were never received. I would send presents for their birthdays and Christmas and she would take them back to the store. I remember one Christmas when I called and I asked one of my daughters if she liked the present I sent her." Texas Dad's daughter responded with, "what present…I didn't get any present from you." Then she said, "Oh that, Mom said that she got that for us."

At the age of seventeen years old, one of Texas Dad's daughters developed leukemia. Texas Dad said, "My ex-wife made it very difficult for me to see her. I thought of trying to get custody of her, but I knew that it would never be granted to me with my daughter being so sick. Even when I called the hospital, they would not give me any information. It took me three days to get permission to see my daughter. I stayed the night with her and we talked. That was the last time I saw her. When she did pass away, my ex-wife did not even call me. I heard about it from her friend. When it comes to his ex-wife, Texas Dad said that it took him a long time to forgive her for all of the pain she has caused him. Texas Dad said that, "I would have felt better about my ex-wife being so mean like she was if I would have beaten her, gone out on her, or done something to make her so bitter and miserable. I didn't do anything, and I refused to do anything to cause the kids to hate her because of me. If they had bad feelings towards her it would be all her own doing. I finally sent her a letter forgiving her for keeping me away from my children and from my daughter when she was dying and many other things."

As far as Texas Dad's relationships with his adult children now, he says that the younger two, who were eight and ten at the time he was forced to leave, have little to do with him. They do call and have been to visit but the relationship is not what Texas Dad would have hoped for. Fortunately, prior to his second oldest daughter's death, they were able to have some conversations about what had happened, why he left, and she died knowing that her dad did love her and that he had very genuine sadness over the lost years they could have shared together. Texas Dad said, "that for a long time I wanted to tell them what happened. I needed them to know what really happened. I couldn't force it, but I wanted them to ask. The middle two were the only ones who seemed to want to know the story." Texas Dad says that his youngest daughter is "very sweet with us" and accepting of her dad's relationship with his partner. In fact, Texas Dad says that his daughter has asked some very good questions such as how he knew that he loved his partner and how he knew he was gay. She asked her dad if he really wanted his children. Texas dad responded with, "I love children and of course I wanted you." Texas Dad commented on how unfortunate it is that many people assume that gay people do not want to be parents."

Texas Dad's daughter's biggest question was why he never called them. Texas Dad then explained that he did call them all the time. He even went so far as to keep records of every phone call and letter sent. Texas Dad said, "I let a friend, or a coworker know each and every time that I sent a letter or made a phone call so that later on my kids would know how hard I tried to stay connected to them. This way, in case they ever asked, there were people who could verify that I really did try to reach them." Though at a certain point, Texas Dad realized that keeping a box full of records into their adulthood was no longer healthy. Looking back, he realized that, "In my mind as a father, I needed to justify me to them. The only way I knew was to keep records. It was my word against their mother's, but if I had records than they would have to realize that I did call."

Much into their adulthood, Texas Dad decided to throw away the two large boxes of records as an attempt to let go. He realized at this point that he needed to let go. Texas Dad explained that hanging on to these records was enabling him to hang on to his old life as well as the emotional pain associated with those years, and not to move forward into his new life. By throwing away these records and writing his ex-wife a lengthy letter of forgiveness, he was able to free himself from a place where he felt "stuck" and unable to move on.

As far as advice for a young adult who may be going through the process of coming to terms with being gay or whether he or she is unsure of their sexuality, Texas Dad suggests that they wait on the idea of getting married. Texas Dad said that at the time he felt that, "I had to give it a chance that getting married could change me. My advice to anyone is not to get married thinking that it will change you because it won't work. You are who you are, and anyone who I have talked to who is gay and tried this thing and so on, has never changed. They had a façade. There are a lot of men who are gay and married, and it is a facade. They are trying to convince themselves that they are straight. You're not. You stand out. There is no way. We know. As a gay person, you know you are gay and that you are going to hurt that person. There is no way that you are not going to hurt that person. It is just the pressure of society, and parents, and church, and family stating that you have to be straight, and then they blame you afterwards because it is your fault that you caused this problem. In fact, a lot of my issues after the divorce when everything was done, with the church and everybody else, was that I felt forced into the whole thing and told that it would change me, and then I was blamed and ostracized because this is who I am." In fact, one of Texas Dad's more painful memories had to do with the bishop of his church. When the bishop found out about Texas Dad's sexual orientation, he responded with, "I don't hate you, but I don't know how to handle this. I can't deal with this."

As far as realizing their sexual orientation, both partners said that they knew very early on even though they may not have had a label for how they felt different from the other boys. Texas Dad's partner disclosed that, "I knew when I was four, but I didn't figure it out until I was sixteen that I was fundamentally different from everybody else. I just knew that I was attracted to other teenage boys, and I thought that it was just a phase and that other people probably went through it, too. I wasn't really worried about it. Then, when the other guys started to get excited about having girlfriends and going to dances, I continued thinking to myself that I was still in this phase. Then I realized that this is no phase. This is who I am." Texas Dad added that, "The funny thing is, both my partner and I had a lot of girlfriends. A lot of girls liked to be around us. It was really difficult being around the boys. I think the reason why, at least for me, is that I didn't want them to figure out that I was gay. We loved being with the girls. It was fun." Texas Dad's partner commented that, "I was uncomfortable with the other guys because I didn't share their interests, their interests in girls and sports. It was primarily those two things. In fact, I went through a very brief period where I decided that I would be straight, so I *acquired* a girlfriend and we went on a date. It just didn't go right at all. I just said to myself that this is so wrong. I can't do this. I would rather be by myself."

As far as being a gay parent, Texas Dad says that ironically, "I was more nurturing than she was. I wanted my kids so much. I knew that she would not take care of them the way I would of. For her, it was all about the money, the child support. I have no doubt that deep inside she knows that the children would have been better off with me, too." Texas Dad went on to talk about everything that he had done with his kids prior to the split. He talked about the father-daughter dates they had every Friday night. Each weekend, one daughter at a time would get to choose where she wanted to go out to dinner. Texas Dad also took them camping and on day trips, and commented that he was the "glue" as far as their life as a family. In fact, he said, "I was the one keeping the family together and working. I had rules, but I was also lenient and understanding when I needed to be. After I left, things very quickly went down hill. I was hearing things from people that never would have happened if I was there."

Texas Dad's partner, on the other hand, though he admits that he never wanted to have his own children, very much enjoys spending time with his grandchildren. He says that for the most part that, "Most gay men don't want kids. I think that the ones that do make good parents because they really want it and they work for it. For straight people it is just kind of the blue print. You're straight, so you get married and have kids. Whether they will be good parents or not, or whether they really *want* children or not doesn't matter. It's just how it is. For gay people, they have to really *want* kids. They have to work for it, and because of this will probably be really good parents." Not only do they have to work for it, Texas Dad's partner says, " but because of all that gay people go through as far as the coming out process, and how we are treated at times, we are often more self aware. I think gay people often have a more solid sense of who they are because of what they have been through." Certainly most psychologists and child development experts would agree that having a solid sense of self, as well as the ability to love and accept oneself is an invaluable asset in the parenting world, and can only benefit both the parent and their child.

Just to take things a step further, to be self-aware as well as *seasoned* can be a great asset to any relationship. I was able to get the take on what it is like to be lesbian grandparents from two New York women who have been together for twenty-four years. The couple never had children together, but one of the part-ners had been previously married and had three children with her ex-husband. When New York Grandma first told her children that she was lesbian, they were seventeen, fourteen, and two years old. When asked how it all went down, New York Grandma responded, "pretty well, actually. My oldest son was upset, but mostly because of the marriage breaking up, not because of me being in a same-gender relationship. As far as my daughter is concerned, it was easier for her than it was when her father got remarried because she did not feel that he was being replaced. Of course the little one was too young to understand what was going on."

When her oldest two children got married, all was smooth for the most part. At her son's wedding, New York Grandma was escorted down the isle with her nephew, then took her rightful place with her partner who had reserved her a seat. At her daughter's wedding, New York Grandma said that she and her partner were announced together and were able "to have more of a roll as a couple." In fact, both new families that her children married into are traditional, Irish-Catholics, with one father-in-law being a retired BCI Investigator and the other retired from the NYPD. New York Grandma said that the couple has always been discreet, and that both new families of in-laws have been very accepting of them.

As far as the grand-parenting piece, New York Grandma's Partner has been there from the beginning so they "never knew anything different." New York Grandma's Partner shared much of the shuttling back and forth to doctor appointments when New York Grandma's kids were younger, then continued her involvement when the grandchildren arrived. New York Grandma's Partner admitted that she was uncomfortable with the "infant stage," and that she followed the cues from New York Grandma. Much of the reason that New York Partner didn't know how to interact with small children, she says, "was because I had very little interaction or affection from my parents growing up. Children were something to be endured until they were old enough to leave the house." New York Partner says that she has taken her parental cues from New York Grandma and says that, "she has had to roll model that for me." According to New York Grandma, her partner has "done an excellent job of step-parenting as well as grand-parenting. Very early on she became involved with the kids, and knew when to stay out of an argument. She stepped in when she needed to, but knew not to parent them too much because their dad was very much in the picture. The kids always knew, however, that they had another adult that they could count on."

In fact, they shared a funny story with me about New York Grandma's youngest. As he was only two years old when her partner entered the picture, as far as he knew, she was always there. By the time he entered college he was certainly very close and comfortable with his mother's partner. It just so happens that he chose to attend a small, private, very artsy school where many of the students were not so *mainstream*. New York Grandma says, "This school attracted very smart, odd children. We arrived at the school and my son wanted to show us around the campus. It was very ethnically diverse. There were a lot of earrings and a lot of tattoos. My tall, skinny, white kid kind of stood out. Before we knew it, he was dragging us around to every single person he had met thus far, introducing us as 'the rents'. It was cute. He couldn't wait to show off his two moms. I think it gave him a certain edge."

They shared another story with me. This one involved the oldest grandchild when she was in first grade. The class was making their family tree, and naturally she included everybody, both grandmas as well as her grandpa and his new wife. The teacher told her that she must have made a mistake, and that she couldn't possibly have three grandmas on one side of the family. The child was adamant of course, that she really did have three grandmas and went home and told her parents. Unfortunately, the child was made to choose which name would be written in the designated space, and was apparently "very incensed about the whole thing."

Telling this story reminded the couple of what it was like back in the early 80's raising three children in a same-sex household. They both said that back then, "there was virtually no support within the lesbian community." New York Grandma then added, "and there were no books. I remember being so excited when eventually things started to be written about same-sex couples and parenting, but it came years later. In the early 80's, there was nothing for us as far as support. I even remember a certain meeting place that we had within our local lesbian community, and male children were not allowed to be there. I also remember a certain lesbian singer who held concerts, and male children were not allowed to attend her concerts. It was hurtful and isolating." New York Grandma remembers having to drive an hour and a half upstate just to attend a conference for same-sex parents. Then New York Grandma commented on how much things have changed. She said, "that it is so much easier now to have children when you are in a same-sex relationship. When we go to Province Town, there are same-sex couples all over the place with children. There is so much more support out there now. It's nice."

New York Grandma sums up with discussing the importance of choosing the right community to live in. She and her partner currently live outside New York. They have found a church that they really like where they feel welcome and accepted. New York Grandma is also involved in a Bible study group that she enjoys very much. The area where they live, for the most part, is open to and accepting of alternate lifestyles. New York Grandma says, "there are many places to live where a same-sex couple can be who they are and be accepted. We feel so lucky to live here. I wouldn't want to try this in some remote place where the ways of thinking are not what we are used to. I just wouldn't want to do that. It is important to be comfortable within your community." And speaking of comfortable, upon winding up our interview, New York Grandma informed me that her youngest son is about to become engaged to a Korean young woman. Apparently, the young woman's parents are a bit uncomfortable with the fact that their daughter will be marrying a young man who is Caucasian. New York Grandma chuckled to herself and said, "they think that's a tough pill to swallow, wait until they find out that their son-in-law-to-be has two moms."

PART VI

On Staying Connected Through These Challenging Years…

20

Surviving the Deep End of the Ocean...

There is probably no more unsettling realization for the parents of teenagers than coming to grips with the reality that all your hard-earned advice, wisdom, and life lessons are falling on deaf ears.

—Michael Riera, Ph.D.
—author of *Staying Connected to your Teenager*

There was a time when I used to whine about all the extra kids in the house, the increased noise level, and the rapidly disappearing batches of chocolate chip cookies. Many people who live in the country get an occasional mouse; however, I was convinced we had an army of them, or worse, a very clever snack thief who washed down his stolen goodies with gallons and gallons of just-paid-for milk. Now that my oldest is a teenager with three tweens right behind him, I no longer complain. I am happy that he wants to be here, and that his friends do also. The extra money spent on Gatorade and pretzels is a small price to pay to know that my teen is safe and sound downstairs with his buddies.

It is also important to know your teen's friends. Teens, of course, are not known for engaging in lengthy conversations, especially if they are spontaneous and during daylight hours, but it is good to try. At least this way, on some level, your teen's friends will get it that you are interested in getting to know them, and more importantly, that you are watching. Sometimes it is not so much what we say or how we say it, but *what we put out there*. By asking a few *by the way* type questions such as how is the soccer season going so far or what's going on in high school these days, will send an *involved parent* signal to your teen's friends.

On the flipside, it is also important not to stick our noses in too far as this is a big *no no* in the teen world. There is a small window for us to work with where we have a handle on what is going on, yet don't push them away by violating teen etiquette. We also want to be wary of the *buddy-buddy syndrome*, which can be easy to slide into. Though it is important to maintain a fairly high level of *cool* so that our teens and their friends will keep the lines of communication open, it is important *not* to send the message that we are all in this together. This is their turn, as we already had a turn to be a teen and hopefully we passed this life-stage with honors. In fact, it is often the teen-life-stage flunkies who get sucked into being one of the gang. Sometimes adults feel comfortable hanging out with their teens and their friends because underneath it all, this is where they are emotionally. For lack of a better way to say it, they are stuck. This is obviously not healthy for either party involved.

When discussing communicating with teenagers, Michael Riera, Ph.D. author of *Staying Connected To Your Teenager*, talks about the complete ineffectiveness of talking *at* our teens, meaning specifically giving lectures and advice. He says that, "Lectures are not very effective for improving your connection to your teenager. The next time you shift into this mode with your teenager, watch him closely. You'll see all of the signs of him dissociating from the moment: eyes fixed in space and glazed over, fidgeting (or the opposite, complete stillness), and slack jaws. In these moments, most teenagers either get angry or check out to another time and place, usually away from the person delivering the lecture. When you notice this happening with your teenager, your best bet is to stop talking. You are going no where fast. Better to cut your losses then and there and hope for a fresh start the next time around." Basically when we give a teenager a lecture, we are talking *at* them with information based on our own vast knowledge and life experience, and applying it to their seemingly minimal knowledge and life experience.

Though the intentions beneath the monotone life narrative may be innocent, on some level the condescending nature of the delivery may be picked up by teen radar. This may also tick them off.

Advice-giving differs from lecture-giving, in that instead of a lesson being thrown at our teen, she is receiving specific help with an isolated problem. This help may be unsolicited, which of course the teen will find equally as irritating as the lecture. The difference also, is that lectures are usually rejected outright, whereas advice can be rejected initially, then after sitting with a teen for a while, may seep in slowly. Riera explains, "It's strange, but just because your daughter rejects your advice does not mean that she ignores it. Once she hears what you have to say and rejects it-either by pointing out what is wrong with what you have to say or by allowing herself to feel insulted by your wanting to control her life-she is free to discover the usefulness of your advice on her own down the road. Yes, the suggestion you made about how to deliver that difficult feedback to her friend was rejected out of hand. But then, two weeks later, she might stumble upon that same idea and attribute it to herself. Now the idea serves her growing autonomy in the world, not her regressed dependence on you. That is, she thinks it is her idea. So when she tells you how she resolved the problem, don't you dare try to reclaim credit for the idea. Instead-smile and nod your head-a lot. Let her show off her independence to you and to take the credit. She will not get a big head from all this, and best of all, the connection between the two of you will grow stronger and deeper."

Riera also explains that following one of these *close moments* that it is not uncommon for our teenager to pick a fight, and once we are aware of what is going on with our teen's need to *start* with us, that things will be better for both parties involved. Riera says that, "Believe it or not, this is a normal reaction after a teenager has taken and successfully used your advice. What's going on is that by soliciting and following your advice, he has made himself unduly dependent on you at a time of life when independence is sacred. The best way he knows to recover from this momentary lapse is to exaggerate his sense of independence, and picking a fight with you and holding his ground (whether he is right or wrong) is the classic way for a teenager to do this. At end of the fight, his sense of independence has been restored." Riera continues to say that, "to add insult to injury, he expects that you know the fight is nothing personal. At least that's how he takes it, which is why an hour later, while you're stewing over the argument, your teenager has moved on without a backwards glance." Riera suggests that once you have experienced one of these moments where your teen has solicited advice and actually allowed it to sink in and put it to use, that as parents we should "expect the exaggerated reclamation of independence through some sort of argument..." Then once the argument is over to, "try as much as you can to see what it is all about-independence-so that you don't take it personally." Furthermore, Riera explains that, "If you can keep your equilibrium through this, then your connection with your teenager grows enormously. He learns that he can count on you to understand what he can't say and doesn't yet understand himself."

It is also important when dealing with teens, or anyone else for that matter, not to make assumptions or to take what they say personally. The very simple truth of the matter is that we never really know what is in someone else's world. We can think we do, and often times we feel that we are positive about what is going on with someone, but the fact is that we are merely guessing. Something could have happened in their day, someone could have said something that went straight to their jugular vein and caused some misplaced anger to leak out sideways. For teens especially, they could be having an insecure moment (which happens frequently throughout their day), and we could have walked in right in the middle of their internal earthquake. Sometimes these tremors can rank high on the emotional Richter scale. While our teens walk around in silence trying to process these uncomfortable feelings, or the opposite, when they are acting out on these shaky teen feelings, we often interpret or smell an attitude in the air.

Don Miguel Ruiz writes in *The Four Agreements* that, "We have the tendency to make assumptions about everything. The problem with making assumptions is that we *believe* they are the truth. We could swear that they are real. We make assumptions about what others are doing or thinking-we take it personally-then blame them and react by sending emotional poison with our word. That is why whenever we make assumptions, we're asking for problems. We make an assumption, we misunderstand, we take it personally, and we end up creating a whole big drama for nothing." Ruiz also talks about giving it our best shot each day. I know that I am often telling our kids simply to do their best, and that we would never be upset with a grade or performance as long as they gave it their best. This also holds true for us grown-ups. Ruiz suggests that, "Under any circumstance, always do your best, no more and no less. But keep in mind that your best is never going to be the same from one moment to the next. Everything is alive and changing all the time, so your best will sometimes be high quality, and other times will not be as good." He continues, "If you try too hard to do more than your best, you will spend more energy than is needed and in the end your best will not be enough. When you overdo, you deplete your body and go against yourself, and it will take longer to accomplish your goal. But if you do less than your best, you subject yourself to frustrations, self-judgment, guilt, and regrets. Just do your best-in any circumstance in your life." For me, these tools of communication are invaluable.

Speaking of communication, it is also a really, really, good idea to listen and talk with your spouse or partner frequently. Go out to dinner. Go on walks. Stay connected. It is important to communicate with your spouse or partner anyway, but especially during the teen years it is so essential to be supportive of each other. No one knows, loves, and understands a child like his or her own parents even if it doesn't feel that way at the moment. There is certainly no one better to bounce concerns and feelings off of than the other parent, or a trusted family member who also knows and loves your child. It is your *inner-circle* people who are best suited to embrace your child's strengths and gifts, even if your teen is in a state of confusion or emotional turbulence. It is also during this stressful time, that we actually benefit from *reducing* our tolerance to stress. The less stress we are willing to accept, the less we will have.

A good barometer for our stress level, other than physical symptoms such as sleeping and eating habits, blood pressure, etc., is the state of our external world. I know for sure that this is true for me. I am certainly no neat freak (as anyone who knows me will attest), however, when my house gets cluttered and things are out of order, I often realize that I *feel* out of order. I may have temporarily taken on too much and may need to makes cuts in my schedule as difficult as that may be. I may have too many thoughts, concerns, or unresolved issues soaring across my mind that may need to be discussed and worked through. All of this mental clutter is cumulative and takes its toll on us. Not only that, but being overwhelmed and out of order also takes its toll on our family, as stressed out people are generally not too much fun to be around. Richard Carlson, PH.D., writes in *Don't Sweat The Small Stuff with Your Family*, to "Keep in mind, as within, so without." He says that the greatest value of this strategy is "to help you regain your perspective when your life seems hectic and out of control. It stems from the understanding that your outer world-your environment, the noise level, the relative calm or chaos in your life-is usually a reflection of your inner world, the degree of peace and equanimity (or lack thereof) you experience in your mind." Basically, we are far more apt to *respond* in a calm and focused manner if we are feeling calm and focused on the inside. When we are frenzied within, we have far more of a tendency to *react* rather than *respond*.

What this means in a nutshell, is to be good to yourself (and you should anyway), by enjoying the simple things. Figure out and do that which makes your heart sing, whether it be painting, hiking, learning Swahili, or taking Irish dance lessons. Self-care also involves carving out a moment of solitude, even if it is exactly that, a moment. There will always be things to do, projects to complete, and piles of laundry in the closet. We need to make alone time a priority if we are going to gain or maintain our sanity and inner peace throughout the teen years. This is a good rule for life in general, but especially during this turbulent time, appreciating the smaller things if life and embracing solitude can be very therapeutic for the spirit. On a more frivolous note, if you can fit a massage in once and a while you will be that much better off as far as the dealing with the daily curveballs. Physical exercise is a must for anyone with teenagers. Not only are you blowing off steam, but this can be used as valuable time to be alone and collect one's thoughts, or as time to be active with friends. Either way, physical exercise will enhance one's emotional well being every bit as much as one's physical well being, not to mention the automatic release of endorphins which naturally elevate feelings of happiness. Endorphins are nature's Prozac.

Much of the reason for our stress, or *anticipated* stress is that the adolescent life-stage is infamous for its challenges, emotional turbulence, and for parental anxiety about no longer being able to control our child's environment. As far as keeping our kids safe, it used to be that we could simply remove sharp objects from their reach and hold their hands crossing a busy road. Now we have to worry about hormones, unprotected sex, and drinking and driving. Sex with protection, ruling out pregnancy, AIDS, or STDs can still be frightening for emotional reasons. As parents, we worry about our teen ending up with someone who is *emotionally* dangerous and the long-term damage that can be done by doing something *adult* that our son or daughter may not have been ready for. The drinking part of our driving fears is of course every parent's biggest nightmare, but I think that most of us would admit that driving all by itself is a scary thought. Thinking about these inexperienced drivers, without the veteran ability to react or drive defensively is enough to keep most of us awake at night. Where we live in Northern Vermont it is dark, very, very, dark. In fact, it is a whole different kind of dark than anywhere else. We have a winter that is eight months long, ice, lots of snow, deer, and an occasional moose. To top it off, the roads are steep and windy, with lots of blind spots. Just the mere thought of our kids driving or being driven on these roads is enough to cause a panic attack.

The worries can also be different for parents in the burbs and cities. They have to worry a little more about accidents with other cars, as there are so many. They have to worry about people running stop signs and traffic lights. We do not have too many traffic lights where we live. We do have our share of drunks though. In rural areas, drunks know that their chances of getting pulled over are minimal so we breed them out here. People in the burbs and cities have to worry more about car-jackings and late-night creeps. We have creeps, too, but not as many so they stand out. In fact the whole town knows who they are so we avoid them. In the burbs and cities, spontaneous interactions with dangerous people are a constant worry for parents.

Speaking of the car, if your teen is still too young to drive solo, then embrace that time. More parents have talked to me about deep conversations that have gone on in the car on the way to Taco Bell or wherever. Sometimes the kids are in the backseat talking about who said or did what with whom, completely forgetting that a parent is in the driver's seat. This is a really good time to keep quiet and listen. Take it all in. Learn about your teen's world and whatever you do, don't bring any of it up unless they do. If they do, then continue to listen. These spontaneous chats with teens can be wonderful and make us feel very good as parents because it reminds us of the old days when we were totally involved in the details of our child's life, however, it is important not to blow it. They want us to be involved in a way, to be connected, yet there is also the part of our teen that is striving to break free and be independent. By talking too much during these moments, or bringing this conversation up again when it is done, can be perceived as a major set back for the teen, as they can feel as if they have fallen off the horse so to speak. Even though the connected feeling with Mom or Dad can feel warm and secure, it may also trigger a feeling of failing to cut loose and be independent. This is why it is good, during these spontaneous chats, to be an extremely good listener and to let the teen have control of when the conversation is over. Bringing it up again the next day is a big *no* for the same reasons. What we need to do is savor the moment, and if we still want or need to talk, then we can share what we want to say with our spouse, partner, or another trustworthy person.

Some of the ways that we stay connected with our teens are different than how we managed when our children were little, but some are not. Our teens still want and need us to be present at sports events and other presentations or performances. We may not need to yell as loud, or wave as much, but being there is very important. They need to know that we care enough about them to manipulate schedules in order to be present at something that is important to them. When we acknowledge what is important to our teen we acknowledge that they are important to us.

It is also a good idea to stay in contact with high school teachers and principals whether your child is a good student or not. Most of us attend parent teacher conferences and open houses all through elementary school. Then, during the middle school years things start to slow down to an occasional meeting, usually following a problematic phone call or concern from a teacher. The routine kinds of open houses slow down. Some schools still have them, but teachers report that the numbers of parents showing up drops dramatically after sixth grade. In high school, after the initial orientation for new parents of high schoolers, there is very little contact with teachers or administration unless it is specifically requested. This is not to say that we should still be making decisions about whether or not our child is going to take metal shop or theatre as an elective, but it is good to at least be aware of his or her choices. Without an awareness of what is going on with their schedules, there obviously can't be any discussion or encouragement. For the parent who has been very hands on throughout their child's life, this can be a huge adjustment. The skill of *loving from a distance*, however, is a skill that can be mastered with practice and patience.

It is also important for us to remember that teens are still very much in need of consistency and limits. Though they are becoming more self-aware and learning to be the masters of their own universes, they still need a few walls to bounce off of in order to figure out who they are, and what it means to be a responsible young man or woman. Though they are making progress as far as their ability to see around corners, they are not there yet, and will benefit from assistance in processing what the results or consequences of an action may be. Even the most levelheaded kids, who are brought up in cohesive, loving family environments, make bad choices, sometimes fatal ones. This is why it is of utmost importance, to process with our teens what the situation *really* is, and what the effects of the external circumstances could mean for them. Especially with social situations, teens often fail to visualize how their environment could become overwhelming. Teens are trying so hard to prove to themselves and the world that they are in control, that they almost feel a sense of failure if they admit that going to a certain party is making them nervous.

Speaking of parties, it is also important to give our teens a *back door policy*, or a way out if the situation does become overwhelming or dangerous. By giving our kids alternative choices, we are empowering them by giving them the tools they may need to survive the night. Many parents in the group that I facilitate have talked about giving their teens money for a cab (or a cab voucher) every night when they go out, just in case the person who drove them there is not in good shape to drive them home. These same parents have also made it clear that their teens can call home at any time of night, *without questions asked,* and they will be picked up. This also goes for their teen's friends. The *without questions* part is a tough one. I know myself that I would want to know what happened. I do, however, think that *some* questions could be asked as long as nobody got blamed or in trouble, as what is important during this life-stage is to keep our kids alive and free from severe life-changing injuries. We want our teen's experience of calling us to be picked up to be a positive one (or at least not negative) so that they would do it again if they had to. We want to be a safe-haven for our kids. In fact, for teens in general, it is very much a good idea to meet them where they *are* instead of *where we want them to be.*

Bibliography

ADHD and Teens, *A Parent's Guide to Making it Through the Tough Years, Proven Techniques for handling Emotional, Academic, and Behavioral Problems,* by Colleen Alexander-Roberts, Foreword by Paul T. Elliot, M.D., Taylor Publishing Company, Copyright 1995

Adolescent Worlds-*negotiating family, peers, and school* by Patricia Phelan, Ann Locke Davidson, Hanh Cao Yu, Teacher's College Press-Columbia University, Copyright 1998, pg. 12.

Beyond Appearance-*a new look at adolescent girls,* edited by Norine G. Johnson, Michael C. Roberts, and Judith Worell, American Psychological Association. Copyright 1999, pgs. 214-215. This book is a compilation of the works of many researchers. Eden (1985) and Merten (1997) were the two researchers quoted on the pages cited. If any other researchers were involved directly or indirectly and were not cited appropriately, I apologize.

Beyond the Big Talk-*Every parents guide to raising sexually healthy teens-from middle school to high school and beyond,* by Debra W. Haffner, M.P.H. Newmarket Press-New York. Copyright 2001, 2002 by Debra Haffner.

Boys and Girls Learn Differently! By Michael Gurian and Patricia Henley with Terry Trueman, pg. 289. Published by Jossey-Bass, a Wiley Company.

Boys to Men: emotional miseducation, by Bridget Murray, The Monitor Online, Volume 30, Number 7 July/August 1999, pg. 2.

Cleared for Takeoff, *50 Ways parents can help teenagers grow up and into lives of their own,* pg. 87, by Wayne Rice, Word Publishing, Nashville. Copyright 2000

Decadence & Objectivity by Lawrence Haworth, University of Toronto Press, pgs.5-7 Copyright 1977.

Driven to Distraction, *Recognizing and Coping with Attention Deficit Disorder from Childhood through Adulthood*, by Edward M. Hallowell, M.D., and John J. Ratey, M.D., pg.70 (quote by Emily Dickinson 1864)

Girlfighting*-betrayal and rejection among girls*, by Lyn Mikel Brown
New York University Press, Copyright 2003

Give Your ADD Teen a Chance, *A Guide for Parents of Teenagers with Attention Deficit Disorder*, by Lynn Weiss, Ph.D., pgs. 137-138, Pinon Press, Copyright 1996.

Growing Pains: The Middle School Years, by Lisa Hayes
Partnership for Learning-Equipping families and communities to maximize learning. (Information derived from the Internet)

Harmful to Minors*-*The Perils of protecting kids from sex, by Judith Levine, foreword by Dr. Joycelyn M. Elders, University of Minnesota Press, Copyright 2002.

'Hookups' and Dating Similar to Teens, by Jennifer Warner, reviewed by Brunilda Nazario, M.D., October 18th, 2002.

Internet Gives Teenage Bullies Weapons to Wound from Afar
By Amy Harmon, New York Times.com, August 26th, 2004

Mirror, mirror*-A summary of research findings on body image*, SIRC, by Kate Fox, 1997. (Information derived from the Internet)

Mixed Messages; *What are We Telling our Gifted Girls?* PTA TODAY 20(4 March/April): 30-31, by Joan F. Smutny (1995) (Information derived from the Internet)

Modernization and Postmodernization*-Cultural, Economic, and Political Changes in 43 Societies*, by Ronald Inglehart, pg. 339, Princeton University Press, Copyright 1997.

Outing Yourself*-How to Come Out As a Lesbian Or Gay To Your Family, Friends, and Coworkers*, by Michelango Signorile, pg. Xxi, Simon and Schuster, Copyright1995.

Real Boys-Rescuing Our Sons from the Myths of Boyhood, by William Pollack, Ph.D., pgs. 306-309 and 321-327. Copyright 1998, Published by Henry Holt and Company-An Owl Book.

Same-sex Marriage & Parenting by April Martin, Ph.D., Psychologist and Executive Vice President of the Gay and Lesbian Coalition International (Information derived from the Internet)

*Schoolgirls-*Young Women, Self-Esteem, and the Confidence Gap, by Peggy Orenstein, Anchor Books, a division of Random House, Inc.Copyright 1995, 2000. Pgs.xx-xxi-introduction.

*Single Fatherhood-the complete guide-*by Chuck Gregg, Ph.D., Sulzberger & Graham Publishing, Ltd., Copyright 1995, pgs. 123-124.

6 Steps to an Emotionally Intelligent Teenager-teaching social skills to your teen, by James Windell. Published by John Wiley and Sons, Inc. Copyright 1999.

Staying Connected To Your Teenager-How to Keep Them Talking To You And Hear What They Are Really Saying, by Michael Riera, Ph.D., Perseus Publishing, Copyright 2003, pgs.59-63.

Supporting Girls in Early Adolescence. ERIC Digest, 1995, by Dianne Rothenburg. (Information derived from the Internet)

The Adonis Complex-How to identify, Treat, and Prevent Body Obsession in Men and Boys by Harrison G. Pope, M.D., Katharine A. Phillips, M.D., and Roberto Olivardia, Ph.D., pgs.xiii, 176-177. Published by Simon and Schuster. Copyright 2000.

The Child, The Family, and the Outside World, by D.W. Winnicott, pg. 116, Perseus Publishing. Copyright 1964.

The Four Agreements-a Practical Guide to Personal Freedom, by Don Miguel Ruiz. Copyright 1997. Amber-Allen Publishing, pgs. 63-64 and 75-76.

The Good Son, by Michael Gurian. Copyright 1999, Tarcher/Putnam Books

The Middle School Years, by Michele Hernandez. (Information taken from excerpts of her chapters from the Internet)

The Myth of Maturity-What Teenagers Need From Their Parents To Become Adults, by Terri Apter, WW Norton & Company Ltd. Copyright 2001 by Terri Apter.

The Romance of Risk-Why Teenagers Do The Things They Do, by Lynn E. Ponton, pgs. 161-162. Published by Basic Books, a member of the Perseus Books Group, Copyright 1997.

The Truth About Tweens, Newsweek, October 18th, 1999-with Karen Springen in Chicago, Ana Figueroa in Los Angeles, and Nicole Joseph-Goteiner in San Francisco, pgs. 62-72.

The Twelve Steps and Twelve Traditions by Bill Wilson Pub by AA World Services, Inc.

Those Middle School Years: Motivation and Achievement begin at home, by Krish and Hannigan, Everything Kids! Division of Ottaway Newspapers, Inc., Danbury, CT.

WebMD Health

WebMD Medical News Archive

www.Asbergerssyndrome.net-information derived from this website for the chapter on Teens and Social disorders

Young and Bipolar, Time Magazine, August 19th, 2002, Jeffrey Kluger with Sora Song, pgs. 39-42.

978-0-595-36561-6
0-595-36561-2

Printed in the United States
35581LVS00006B/1-75

9 780595 365616